focus
mind
_ light
up your life

Nichiren Buddhism 4.0

Susanne Matsudo-Kiliani
and Yukio Matsudo

C000139541

COPYRIGHT AND DISCLAIMER

Contents

Foreword

The Japanese Buddhist monk Nichiren (1222-1282) established the innovative practice of *chanting Daimoku*, which is *reciting the mantra of Nam-myō-hō-ren-ge-kyō to a Mandala*. His deepest desire was to empower us to live as the true creators of our own lives and to establish peace in the society we live in. Everyone should be able to enjoy a life where their desires are fulfilled and where they are free from any form of suffering. Thus, this practice can be characterized by its unique orientation towards a proactive commitment to your own happiness as well as the happiness of others.

On a personal level, the fulfilment of our desires is an expression of our true nature which is to open up more creative possibilities for ourselves and others. It turns out that to deny oneself including one's deepest desires is to deny one's true nature.

Nichiren reassures us that "no prayer will go unanswered." And indeed, millions of Nichiren Buddhist practitioners worldwide have experienced miraculous and wonderful benefits such as overcoming serious illness, gaining financial fortune and transforming relationships. Yet, have you ever wondered how such amazing experiences are possible just by the apparently simple practice of chanting Daimoku to the Gohonzon? We wanted to explore the reason why Nichiren had such an unshakeable conviction that all prayers to the Gohonzon will be answered.

We demonstrated the "astonishing effects of the power of Daimoku" by showing the positive changes in our physical energy in our book, *Nichiren Buddhism 3.0,* and by describing the changes to our brainwaves in the following book, *Nichiren Buddhism 3.1.* Now we seek to elucidate the "miracle mechanism" with respect to the question as to why our prayers can be answered. In order to do so, we started a new 4. series which consists of three volumes.

The present book *Nichiren Buddhism 4.0* is the first of three volumes in this series and focuses on the Mandala Gohonzon which Nichiren specifically created for us to fulfill our desires. In this respect we will explain its basic structure and the function of its integrated elements in so far as Nichiren himself emphasized their significance by highlighting them in the Gohonzon. Understanding the radically innovative construction of the Mandala itself should help you to gain a deeper access to the Gohonzon and thereby should provide you with a much deeper understanding of its fundamental meaning.

In order to support this comprehensive analysis, we considered it advisable to translate some traditional Buddhist terms and concepts into the contemporary language of science. In particular, we will focus on traditional Buddhist terms such as "Buddha nature" and "enlightenment". Nichiren himself went beyond their traditional meaning related only to a "buddha" in the sense of a special person. Rather, he expanded these fundamental concepts to the universal foundation of all life and of the world itself. In this respect the term "Buddha nature" can best be understood as "cosmic pure consciousness."

Likewise, you come to understand that "enlightenment" is intrinsically related to "light." Nichiren speaks of his practice as the "Buddhism of the sun" as it is directly associated with the phenomenon of light. He tells us that Daimoku is the light which illuminates our life and transforms our suffering. Actually, this is literally the case in a very modern scientific sense. For you will discover the fascinating nature of the energy we generate when we chant Daimoku. Indeed, Daimoku creates light energy consisting of biophotons.

Since consciousness and light energy are the foundation of life itself and of the universe, the miracle mechanism inherent to

Nichiren Buddhist practice can best be fundamentally explained in terms of light energy and consciousness.

This same light energy is that which is transferred into a concrete, material form in the process of manifesting your visions and intentions. Research demonstrates that your thoughts and intentions are energetic in nature and consist of a stream of biophotons. Consequently, chanting Daimoku with a specific intention will set this miracle mechanism in motion so that you can fulfil your personal vision.

To understand this process, you will be asked to go beyond a materialist view of life and the universe and to pay more attention to the energetic dimension of the reality in which you live. Based on this paradigm shift, the notion *Myōhō* will be explained in terms of the two sides of energy and matter. You will see that your energetic state can tell you more about your health condition than your physical state. Furthermore, it is your mind that influences your body.

You will also understand that your mental state and your own intention are important factors that can decide your destiny and drastically improve your life situation. In this respect quantum mechanics tells us that it is the "observer" himself whose act of observation itself leads to the collapse of quanta like electrons and photons from their energetic state into a material state. This demonstrates that the process of materialization is triggered by an intentional mental act itself.

You will learn about the power of intention and the ways in which you can use it to shape your life. This will enable you to reinforce your intention to live proactively and do your best to fulfil your desires. Through the intensive practice of "focusing your mind," you can start to "design your life" in a pro-active and powerful way.

We have often been asked how we can actually become one with the Gohonzon when our minds are restless and tense. You will find out that the way we pay attention while chanting plays a critical role in being able to reach a state in which we can lower our brainwaves and get into a union with the Gohonzon. You will learn to switch from a narrow focus to a more open focus that allows you to be in a more relaxed, yet very alert mode of attention that enables you to merge with the Gohonzon.

The Gohonzon has also been called a "happiness producing machine." However, in order to achieve happiness, you need a clear vision and intention about what you want to achieve. This book will present you with a clear blueprint which will help you to find out what it is that you really want in life in order to manifest it with the power of Daimoku.

This book was mainly written from the perspective of Susanne Matsudo-Kiliani, with Yukio Matsudo as co-writer contributing his deep and extensive knowledge of Nichiren Buddhism.

We'd like to say a big thank you to Nigel Wray, who was responsible for amending and correcting our initial draft of the English text. And to Alan Ruskin, who was kind enough to carefully edit the preface. We are also most grateful to Lisa Kossoff, for helping us to make the text less opaque and more immediately intelligible. And we also especially thank Traecy Berryman, who has designed the book cover with great artistry and subtle grace (http://www.traecy.com/).

Last but not least, we are deeply grateful to all our readers and friends, many of whom have demonstrated their enthusiastic support for our work with inspiring reviews and warm-hearted posts, both on Amazon and on social media, such as Facebook.

Susanne Matsudo-Kiliani and Yukio Matsudo

Chapter 1
No prayer will be unanswered

The prayers offered by a practitioner of the Lotus Sutra will be answered just as an echo answers a sound, as a shadow follows a form, as the reflection of the moon appears in clear water, as a mirror collects dewdrops, as a magnet attracts iron.

On Prayer, WND I: 344

Chanting in order to fulfil your desires

In 1997 I met an American Nichiren Buddhist who introduced me to his practice. He told me that I could achieve anything by chanting Daimoku. He also explained to me that I could shift my inner world and improve my life situation tremendously because I could transform any negative situation into a joyous event by carrying out this practice. I was intrigued. "How fascinating, that sounds great!", I thought. For the first time in my life I had a real means to change my life in a concrete way. I was impressed and began to chant immediately.

Later on, I heard people say that chanting Daimoku is like a wish fulfilling jewel and that my "desires would lead to enlightenment". "Wait a minute!", I thought. "Our desires lead to enlightenment?" Until then I used to practice a Tibetan form of meditation and knew that desires are generally regarded as the very cause of suffering in Buddhist teachings. Therefore, I considered any ego-based desire as something that needed to be overcome but never to be encouraged.

I could only make some sense of this statement when I found out that this concept was a characteristic feature specific to Nichiren Buddhism.

In this respect it is completely different from all other forms of Buddhist teaching. Our desires can indeed be the driving force enabling us to live a pro-active life. For they lead us to chant intensively in order to create the reality we would like to experience.

It was the practice of chanting Daimoku in order to fulfil our desires which had most fascinated me. What really astonished me when I started chanting Daimoku was the practice of setting a new goal and envisioning a new situation whilst chanting to the Gohonzon, thereby actually manifesting and experiencing it.

Nichiren required that there be "actual proof" of this practice. It was important to set goals and definite wishes that we would like to have realized. Could the practice of chanting Daimoku in front of the Gohonzon really help me to "collapse" and "materialize" electrons into a new actuality or experience in my life as in quantum physics?

At that time, I realized that I had very definite wishes of which I had not even been aware. I had previously pushed many wishes aside, because I had believed somehow in my subconscious mind that I always needed to fight hard for everything and that the beautiful things in life were difficult to achieve.

As my practice of chanting Daimoku progressed, however, I could not suppress the force of my wishes any longer. I became more consciously aware of what my needs and longings actually were.

Chanting Daimoku showed me that I am a creative being.
I realized that you deny the very ground of your being
by denying yourself your true needs.

When I felt a strong desire with respect to a particular area of my life, it became clear to me that I could no longer deny my own dissatisfaction with myself. For the desire for change would become so strong that I just had to do something. But since I had started to chant, I noticed powerful changes to my environment. I felt that my energy had been transformed.

> The Buddhist practice of chanting Daimoku marked
> a turning point from feeling as a victim
> to becoming the creator of my life.

Taking the initiative in my own life

My energized state of life had actually led to the manifestation of new experiences. I began to notice that many events came to me, as Nichiren expressed it, like *"a magnet attracts iron."* This included not only the delightful events that appeared in my life, but also the awareness that every person and thing which no longer fit energetically to my new state of life had disappeared. This included people, work situations, the way I was living, thoughts and feelings. Suddenly I saw very clearly which friendships were no longer good for me. For a while this was also very painful as at first everything familiar seemed to vanish, collapse and break down.

Case study 1:   Chanting for a nice sports car

This even applied to the car I had at the time. When I started chanting, I was driving an old car that annoyed me because its generator broke down at least once a month. I had to have it repaired all the time. Four weeks later, I had the same problem again. It was like being bewitched. I was tired of driving a car that was constantly in need of repair. This dissatisfaction increased my determination to find a nicer and better quality car for myself. I actually began chanting for a new car.

I talked about this to a friend of mine who thought that was very strange. Later on, she said to me: "Well, I have to admit, since you started chanting, a lot of things are happening in your life." This was indeed somewhat strange. In a few months, I managed to improve my financial situation so that I could afford exactly the car I wanted.

At the beginning I did not even know exactly what kind of car I wanted. But then, by talking to a friend about it and by looking

> and comparing, I ended up knowing exactly what kind of car I wanted. A Mazda sports car in British racing green. This is exactly what I ended up buying for a very good price.

I wanted a radical change to the reality I was facing at that time. It was more about being alive and joyful and imagining something which excited me. At the time, this was imagining possessing a sports car which I turned into actuality. I realized the car was really just a by-product of my new state of being. It was not so much about the car itself but rather that I started to care about how I myself felt. Chanting Daimoku made me feel good. I started to generate an energy of joy in my life. And I realized that when I feel good, I get the things I want in actuality far quicker and in much better ways than I could have imagined. It was not just about going out and doing something new, it was about a new state of *being*. Only when I was in that new state, could I really enjoy the material things in my life. I became aware that happiness is not about the accumulation of external things, it is an internal state of being that must be generated from within. It is not just about the actual material manifestations, but also about the wonder and pleasure in the creative process itself.

However, this was only the beginning, and over time, I realized that the power and energy of my consciousness which I could enhance by chanting Daimoku, did not only transform my dissatisfaction with a dysfunctional car. For the power of Daimoku was able to positively transform and alleviate suffering deep within me, as well as deep within other people.

I saw people overcoming cancer by chanting Daimoku, finding the relationship they were looking for, getting a new job and other surprising phenomena.

Chanting for others

Case study 2:   Praying for my sick aunt

I realized this the first time when I began chanting for my aunt who at the time was in a hospital fighting for her life in the final stages of stomach cancer. One day her sister, my other aunt, told me that she had been in a really miserable state that day. I had just begun the practice of "chanting for someone else". That evening I tried it and chanted deeply for one hour to bring relief to my aunt. I visualized that she was feeling better and that her pain would subside. The next day her sister called me to tell that surprisingly my aunt had felt much better the day before. This really moved me deeply.

Had my chanting actually affected her physical state? Could I affect somebody else's physical state even though that person was 200 kilometers away? Did the power of my Daimoku transcend such a distance? How could Daimoku have an effect across such a distance? Were we really connected in such an intimate way?

Realizing your vision

Returning again to the realization that my practice of chanting Daimoku could suddenly create new experiences, circumstances, things and situations from nothing, I became more determined to become clear within myself as to that which I wanted and so to work towards it. At the same time, chanting to attain my deepest wishes and desires seemed to create a mighty flux of energy attracting a beneficial outcome. I began to realize that unseen benevolent forces and support were all around me and assisting in the attainment of my goals. Everything was inter-connected. In many cases, I had the most amazing experiences: "By coincidence" I was at the right place at the right time to meet the very people that were important to the realization of my wishes. I was often amazed by such events, which can be termed a "mystical coincidence of synchronicity". Yet in my situation at the beginning of my practice it had been most important for me to get a better car and a better job.

Case study 3: Getting a job

I remember well when we came back from our visit to Japan in 2012, I once again had the deep wish to present seminars for a company that is located close to where I live.

Once you have lived abroad for a while you lose your business contacts. Thus, coming back from Japan, I realized that I had to build my contacts up from scratch. I had presented seminars at this company before I went to Japan, but in the meantime the personnel manager of that company had changed, and I did not know the new manager.

One day I just chanted to be able to return to my old company to present seminars once again. That day my husband and I went to town to do some shopping. On our way back to the car we passed a shoe shop and my husband decided to look for some sports shoes. Then he changed his mind and we continued walking. Yet I had the strange feeling that we should go back and have a look for shoes. It was a really strong urge which I could not easily explain. I suddenly turned around and told my husband that I wanted to go back to the shop to look for shoes. He agreed and we went back.

To my surprise, in that shoe shop I met someone from the company I was trying to get into. It was one of the managers who had attended my seminars for years and we had always got on very well. I told him that I had just returned from Japan and that I was trying to return to the company but that the personnel manager had changed. It was very difficult to make any contact without a personal reference. He told me to call the personnel manager and gave me the personnel manager's number and that I should use him as my personal reference. That's exactly what I did. This opened the door for me to get back in to the company.

It still took a lot of effort and patience, yet if I had not met this former seminar participant on that day, I would never have succeeded in getting back into the company. I could refer to him when calling the personnel manager. What a coincidence? I could have not planned the occasion of our meeting as easily as this. This outcome gave me a deep sense of being guided and protected. My higher self had been at work once again.

This was only the beginning, though. It took me another two years before finally getting back into the company. The personnel manager made it really difficult for me. He invited me for an interview and then promised to call me back two months later. When he did not call back, I really had to struggle to overcome my pride and my feelings of disappointment and resolve to call him again. He then let me wait time after time, as he appeared to be very insecure about presenting a new training concept to the executives of the various departments.

After a year he invited me to give a talk in front of all the executives of the company. He wanted to get their feedback first before he finally took me on. I had to be persistent and persevere during that time and not give up. I was very nervous to give a talk in front of all the executives, but in the end, it turned out fine. During those months, however, I had to keep up my spirit by chanting Daimoku. That's when I understood that setting a goal and realizing an intention is not only about getting a beneficial outcome. The most important thing is who we become in the process. Are you able to overcome some aspect of yourself which would normally hinder you in seeking to attain your goal? This can be a feeling of insecurity, a lack of perseverance or your own self-agonizing doubts, for instance.

The synchronicity I experienced gave me the chance to start the job, but then I had to work on it and develop patience and persistence. In the end, it took me two years to get the contract. Today I am still giving seminars to that company on a regular basis.

Many experiences such as this made me realize that it had been my definite clear inner intention and determination which had actually transformed not just myself deep within but also the corresponding external circumstances.

After being given the chance to fulfil your desires, you are challenged to continue your effort both in chanting Daimoku and in giving your best to accomplish the task.

Daimoku is the foundation of your daily life

There was also another aspect about chanting Daimoku that was completely new to me. Previously, I had never connected my daily life to my meditation. Now I was taught to consider my work as being part of my Buddhist practice. Everything I experienced on a daily basis was a part of my practice. This aspect "to regard your work and daily life as a Buddhist practice" was determined by Nichiren clearly in the following Gosho:

> If you continue living as you are now, there can be no doubt that you will be practicing the Lotus Sutra twenty-four hours a day. Regard your service to your lord as the practice of the Lotus Sutra. This is what is meant by "No worldly affairs of life or work are ever contrary to the true reality."
> I hope you will deeply consider the meaning of this passage.
> *Reply to a Believer*, WND I: 905

The recipient of this letter was a samurai, exactly like Shijō Kingo, who was serving his lord and was facing a difficult situation, presumably because he had embraced Nichiren's new teaching. Against this background, Nichiren advised him to consider his service to his lord as a Buddhist practice, which is equivalent to managing one's job in accordance with chanting Daimoku. The practice of chanting Daimoku should be considered the foundation of all worldly matters including the peace of the land in which you live in. This was highlighted by Nichiren in the following way:

> When the skies are clear, the ground is illuminated. Similarly, when one knows the Lotus Sutra, one understands the meaning of all worldly affairs.
>
> *The Object of Devotion for Observing the Mind*, WND I: 376

Chanting Daimoku is the foundation upon which to manage your daily activities and forms the basis for peace in the world.

Cleaning your six senses

Concerning the aspect of "regarding your work as a Buddhist practice", Nichiren frequently quotes Tiantai´s commentary to chapter 19 of the »Profound Meaning of the Lotus Sutra« with respect to "the benefits of purifying the six senses." What does it mean exactly to purify the six senses? I often asked myself this question. I discovered that this aspect is indeed very significant for happiness as it influences how one feels within and how one perceives one's particular circumstances.

For you never just see the objects that surround you as they are in themselves, as what you see is always interpreted by certain concepts and dispositions found in your ego consciousness. What you see is also distorted by old unresolved emotional experiences. Essentially by everything you have ever experienced. I observed this phenomenon in a woman I know whose mother had died when she was a very young girl. This must have been such a traumatic event for as a grown-up woman she can never trust anybody. She is always very skeptical and doubts what anybody says. She is always looking for some fault the other person might have or for some weakness or failing in anybody she begins a friendship with. In this way she demonstrates to herself that she can never trust anybody. From the outside, I can see clearly that she is afflicted by a distorted perception of other people which makes her really unhappy.

If your mind is deluded and confused by the influence of your past karma, you perceive everything according to such a pattern of perception. You hear what you want to hear and may tend to misunderstand what somebody else is telling you. If you have the tendency to worry all the time, for instance, then this tendency stops you from enjoying life and all the conspicuous benefits you get like a new car, a new house, a new job or a new relationship. An inconspicuous benefit is when you realize that nothing really worries you anymore because you have developed deep faith in the Gohonzon, and you know that you can positively transform any situation.

To chant Daimoku to the Gohonzon does not only mean to fulfil your desires or to turn a particular intention into an actuality. For there is no point in just fulfilling your wishes if you cannot enjoy what you have attained. Do you recall that our measurements revealed an immense increase in the energy field around your body after chanting Daimoku? This is the creative life force running through your energy field after chanting Daimoku. From an energetic point of view, all your desires and intentions need to flow with this creative life force in order to be brought into reality. Energetically speaking, so to speak, this flow can be blocked by the stagnation caused by dissipated or distorted energy due to various unresolved emotional experiences. According to the German physicist Dr. Michael König, who is undertaking research into the relationship between mind and matter, your grief, your sorrow, your hopelessness, your doubts, your self-denial, your feelings of being trapped, all this can create a stagnation of energy in your energy field which blocks the manifestation of your desires and intentions. It basically depends on you as to how much you block the creative energy life force pulsing through you. Chanting Daimoku can dissolve such energetic blocks. I experience this when I open myself up fully to allow the creative energy of Daimoku flow through my body and energy field, and my old habitual emotional blocks get purified. Once this happens, I might feel the original emotion once more, yet it is afterwards dissolved.

Consequently, if you have the tendency to be depressed or to feel lonely or to withdraw within yourself you cannot enjoy a new house or a new friendship or a new job. In this case, to clean your senses is actually the biggest benefit of chanting Daimoku rather than fulfilling any particular desire or realizing any particular intention.

I clearly saw this with some friends of ours. They really have everything one could imagine and chant for. He has a fantastic job where he earns more than € 10 000 a month. They have a wonderful house with a swimming pool, lovely children, two cars, a supportive circle of friends, a big family. And yet, he is dissatisfied all the time, feels exhausted and depressed, distances himself from his family and just feels unhappy within himself. All the things he has are not really fulfilling to him. This example showed me that happiness is an inside job and depends on being connected with this invigorating flow of life energy. It also showed me how important it is to clean your senses with Daimoku in order to actually enjoy the benefits attained through chanting.

Sometimes it might happen that we chant for something and yet it does not come about. In such a case I often realized that what I wanted was probably not the best solution for me. However, in the end my perception of reality became clearer and more focused, and I experienced the world as a safe and wonderful place once again and I felt much better than before.

Thus, the purification of the six senses means to purify the stagnated energy of unresolved emotions in your energy field. It means to clean your energy field of old wounds that distort your perception and block the manifestation process of your desires and intentions. This is the only thing which can guarantee you a happy life. Only when your perception is clear of past traumas, depression or painful events, can you really appreciate and deeply enjoy all the beautiful occasions and relationships in your life.

When we clearly express our wishes, intentions and desires, we can attain both a clearly manifested, conspicuous benefit and a latent, invisible, inconspicuous benefit. The purification of the six senses can therefore be seen as an inconspicuous benefit which plays a decisive role in creating a happy and fulfilled life. This kind of benefit can also lead to many wonderful experiences.

> Concerning prayer there is conspicuous prayer and conspicu-
> ous response, [...] inconspicuous prayer and inconspicuous re-
> sponse, [...]. But the only essential point is that, if you believe
> in this sutra, all your desires will be fulfilled in both the present
> and the future.   *Letter to the Lay Priest Dōmyō*, WND I: 750

The above-mentioned aspect of purifying the six senses is also an indication of how deeply the effects of practice affect the core of our life. This is a process which constantly takes place while we are striving to fulfill our desires. In this way, we develop good fortune and better conditions for living the life we really want to live. As Nichiren states in this passage, the essential point in order to fulfill our desires is to believe in the power of chanting Daimoku to the Gohonzon.

Your vision gets realized quickly

After many years of chanting Daimoku I realized that I had fulfilled many intentions and desires which I had held in my mind while chanting. Unlike the job opportunity for which I had to work for two years, recently I experienced a different case where an image held in my mind became reality very quickly.

Case study 4:   An unexpected present

> We live in a three-story house and have our main kitchen in the
> dining room on the ground floor. The upper floor is mainly used
> for working at home while it has an additional space for a

second kitchen so the upper floor itself can be turned into a discrete apartment. Since we do not need more than one kitchen, this space on the upper floor has always remained empty. However, this made the whole upper floor seem uncomfortable as if it had not been completed.

One day after chanting Daimoku, I passed this space and thought to myself: "It would be really nice if there was a kitchen in this place. This would make the whole space look cozier." I don't like any modern style of kitchen, but I have always loved kitchens of the white country-style kitchen. This type of kitchen, however, is very expensive because it is usually made of real wood and not from artificial plywood panels. Thus, it was just a feeling I had that it would be nice although unrealistic to have another expensive kitchen upstairs.

Exactly one day later, we got a call from our Vietnamese craftsman who had helped us refurbish the house in the summer and who had become our good friend. He asked if we were interested in a kitchen set as one of his customers was going to replace his old model with a completely new kitchen. I thought to myself: "That sounds great, but I don´t suppose they would give away a white country-style kitchen." Nevertheless, my husband asked him to send us some pictures of the kitchen. And that´s what he did.

A white country-style kitchen was presented to us

When I saw the picture on my husband´s smart phone I could not believe what I was seeing: a white country-style kitchen! I realized that cosmic consciousness, a higher mind, had reacted almost immediately to the image in my head. Within a few days our friend brought the kitchen to install and refurbished it for us. It felt like I had already observed this kitchen into reality.

These are some of my experiences in which I attained benefits (*kudokus*) as a result of the practice of chanting Daimoku. Whenever I think about them, it occurs to me that each time I was challenged to overcome the passive mindset of feeling like a victim or feeling discouraged. I became determinedly proactive in expressing my desires and, consequently, in shaping my own life. This process requires you to free yourself from limiting habits and from a pessimistic mindset. I came to the conclusion that is most definitely the key meaning of the phrase "desires lead to enlightenment".

Exercise

What is the most important benefit you have received since you began chanting Daimoku?

What was this benefit with respect to?

When and where did you receive this benefit?

How was the process of realization?

From what condition did you begin?

How much effort did you put into this, and what was the struggle
you had to overcome?

_ _

What was the result?

_ _

What did you learn from this experience?

_ _

_ _

Chapter 2
Visions create reality

My vision became a reality

I realized that when we chant Daimoku we grow through different phases on a path of progressive development. Sometimes a vision will take only a day to emerge, sometimes it will take weeks or months before we realize our visions. Sometimes it will take years before we change a certain aspect within ourselves so that our vision can become reality.

I realized that the images I was holding in my mind had a tendency to spontaneously become reality, some quickly and others slowly. I asked myself what the reason was that some images appeared slowly while other images appeared to manifest overnight? I have become especially aware of this aspect during the past year as an image I had been holding in my mind quite literally became true. To explain further:

I really hate the cold and especially the grey, foggy, cold and wet weather which tends to be prevalent in Germany in winter. I dreamed of escaping this cold environment and of escaping to a warm country. I must admit that I was also searching for more warm-hearted human relationships, as people tend to be more matter of fact and far less emotional in Germany. I felt a lack of warmth generally.

By coincidence, this picture was lying on the desk next to my *butsudan* (altar). The wonderful picture of a beach with white sand really inspired me every time I chanted. Whenever I glanced at the picture, I could almost feel the white sand under my feet and the warm sunshine on my body. Then things suddenly began to develop in a very particular direction. Coincidences and synchronicities drew us to Mexico.

By February we were as usual, fed up with the cloudy and dreary weather in Germany and at first we thought of flying to Thailand so we might relax and find new energy under the sun.

However, at about the same time, my husband Yukio received a Facebook friend request from an old Japanese friend now living in Mexico-City. He used to study in Germany almost 30 years ago and he knew Yukio well. They started to communicate via messenger and he offered to have our books translated into Spanish because he wanted to make a contribution to Kosenrufu, the propagation of Nam-myō-hō-ren-ge-kyō in order to foster World Peace, in the country where he was now living. His son is a professional translator and he agreed to undertake this task and began to translate our books. Yukio´s old friend also invited us to come and stay with him at his home in Mexico City.

At the same time, my cousin Sandy from California planned to spend a holiday with her husband and some friends in the resort area of Cancún in Mexico. So, for both of these reasons, we decided suddenly to fly to Mexico to meet up with Sandy and Yukio´s friend. Everything was falling into place even though we had decided to take this trip spontaneously, at very short notice. Every-

thing was connected to everything else.

When we arrived at the hotel in Cancún, I was very surprised. I suddenly realized that my dream had come true. The beach and the surroundings looked very much like the image I had always had next to me while I had chanted over the previous months.

As you can see from the picture taken from our hotel in Cancún, the sand is exactly like that I had seen on the calendar picture every day. White, soft sand, the blue sky, the beach and even the palm trees seemed identical to those in the calendar picture.

It was as though something or someone had drawn me to Mexico in order to actually experience that very image which I had continuously held in my mind while chanting.

Be true to yourself

Over the years, I have become aware that for many people, it is not so easy to realize what it is they really want. Sometimes this is the most difficult thing of all. I have realized that some people actually feel uneasy about their desires or that they even feel guilty when they suddenly start to feel more joy or happiness in their life: fear can sometimes block this new joyful state of being. Maybe this is because they think that they are taking something away from others. Yet nothing could be further from the truth. For the more you receive, the more everyone else receives: the more you receive, the more resources you have to help others and to share those resources with them. Ultimately, however, I realized clearly that it was especially important to be in the right state of being while chanting. Was I reliant solely on my own ego, drawing exclusively on my own will power? Or was I reliant essentially on the power of a universal intelligence while chanting? But to begin with, you must really know what it is that you actually want.

Many people frequently complain to me for hours on end that they are dissatisfied with the place they live, with their partner, or with their job. They will tell me how their financial situation leads to frustration on a daily basis. Others are desperate because they have no job or cannot find a partner. I have often noticed that when I then ask the question: "What exactly do you want at this moment"? that this is precisely the moment when it becomes clear that deep down, they are often fearful of having any concrete wishes.

Clear vision can create a new reality. Yet if you never dare to articulate a particular vision, it is as if you are not telling your taxi driver exactly where you want to go.

Case study 5:   I couldn't even imagine being successful

Even people who have been chanting for years, sometimes have trouble acknowledging their deepest desires. Once we did an exercise in our workshop on the topic of success. It turned out that one of the participants could not even imagine being successful. As soon as he thought about it, all of his self-doubts and negative beliefs rose to the surface as though triggered deep within him by the very word "success". Deep down, he felt guilty when he tried to imagine that he could indeed be "successful." He became aware that the beliefs he grew up with rated "successful people" as "negative" or "dishonest or corrupt." Thus, he felt guilty at the prospect of becoming rich and successful". Another person told us with firm conviction: "Yes, good and spiritual people should be humble and poor, but never successful and rich". All these biased beliefs actually prevented them from even imagining themselves as successful.

Deep down their "prayer", that is their deepest wishes and intentions, could never tolerate the thought of being successful, as they believed that a successful person could never be a good person.

Though they had been chanting for many years, they were denying themselves any joy in their lives and weren't happy with their families. Consequently, they needed to become aware of the negativity of their habitual beliefs which had been internalized since childhood. They had to learn to be more honest with themselves and appreciate and cultivate the deep wish to become truly successful and happy, not only for themselves but for their families.

Case study 6:   I am not allowed to be honest to myself

In another workshop we presented, we used to conduct exercises which we had also formulated in our books. We asked our participants to tell us what they really wanted to realize in their lives. One participant whose name was Stefan, told us that it would be very selfish to focus on his own desires and wishes first, before even considering the needs, desires and wishes of his family or of other people. Later, when we took a walk together in the forest near our house, Stefan suddenly had an outburst and his long-suppressed feelings poured forth. At this moment, he knew exactly what he did *not* want anymore. "I don't want to live in this town anymore", he screamed. "I am fed up with the house I am living in – it is so very cold in winter. I just want to get out".

Later on, Stefan admitted that he feared losing his wife if he expressed his wishes and feelings clearly, because he knew that she definitely did not want to leave the house nor the town they were living in.

Stefan really was facing a dilemma. He thought that if he did not meet his wife's expectations they would eventually break up. However, in the end, his false compromise led to exactly what he had feared the most. His wife left him, and his marriage broke down. His daughter began to have severe psychological problems. None of them were happy with their situation.

I learned much from this episode. It became very clear to me that your focus should be on what you really would like to experience, on what you want and on what makes you happy and not on what you are dissatisfied with or on what you don't want. You have to be honest with yourself.

> Chanting Daimoku actually enables you to become honest
> with yourself and to stop denying yourself.
> You have to maintain your clear vision.

Did this mean that I could transform my inner desires and intentions into actualities? That I could change my outer world by changing my inner world first?

Sometimes people try to change their world while they remain inwardly the same. But this is not possible. We may attain things in our lives only through mental focus, yet we will never keep them unless we overcome our limited ego-consciousness and expand our awareness and allow ourselves to unfold and evolve. This is what the practice of Daimoku is all about. After having achieved many goals, I have realized that in the end it is not about a new car, wealth, health, a new job or relationship: it is who we have become during the process. Which aspect of ourselves must we overcome in order to attain and maintain that which we have achieved? How much can we expand our consciousness and elevate our state of life?

Up until that point, I had always thought the opposite. I had thought that once my outer world changed, once I had a new job or a nice vacation or a particular house or relationship, then my inner world would be changed, and I would be happy. Yet, Daisaku Ikeda teaches us exactly the opposite:

> When we change, the world changes. The key to all change is in our inner transformation—a change of our hearts and minds. This is human revolution. We all have the power to change. When we realize this truth, we can bring forth that power anywhere, anytime, and in any situation.   *Human Revolution*

It took me a long time to understand that this statement should be taken quite literally.

Exercise

What would your life look like if you did not have any wishes, dreams and goals?

Right this minute – what is it that you really want? What would you like to experience?

Get clarity on what you really want - imagine a year from now – what does that look like? What would you like to let go of?

And how will you feel then?

Is there something you really would like to have but deep down you think that you cannot reach it?

Can you completely trust cosmic consciousness to lead to the fulfilment of your wishes?

Everything depends on our faith

Sometimes I asked myself why something I had chanted for had not come about yet. Nichiren himself must have been confronted with this question. However, he had a clear answer to it. Nichiren proclaims that no prayer of the practitioner of the Lotus sutra remains unanswered. In addition, he also explains the essential aspect necessary in order to fulfil your desires and intentions while chanting: Our faith alone determines whether our prayers will be fulfilled.

> Whether or not your prayer is answered will depend on your faith; [if it is not] I will in no way be to blame.
>   Clear water can reflect the moon on the surface also clearly. [...] Your minds are all like the water. Weak faith is like muddy and dirty water, while pure faith is like clearly beautiful water.
>   *Reply to the Lay Nun Nichigon*, WND I, p. 1079

The Lay nun Nichigon had sent offerings to Nichiren and had asked him to pray for her particular wishes. He conducted a ceremonial ritual including chanting Daimoku in front of a Mandala Gohonzon and "reported about it to the gods of the sun and the moon." He then gave her some clear guidance, stating that she should take full responsibility for fulfilling her own wishes by developing "pure faith". In the same way, Nichiren advised Nichigen-nyo, the wife of Shijō Kingo, to develop "strong faith".

> As for your wife's prayers, even though she does not doubt the Lotus Sutra, I suspect that her faith may be weak. [...] If her prayers haven't been answered, it is like a strong bow with a weak bowstring, or a fine sword in the hands of a coward. It is in no sense the fault of the Lotus Sutra.

Strong faith is like a strong bow with a strong bowstring

The Royal Palace, WND I: 488

Chapter 3
The wish-granting jewel

Nichiren's unshakable conviction in the power of Daimoku

I quite vividly remember the woman I used to chant with a lot when I started this practice in Heidelberg in 1997. She had overcome multiple sclerosis and many other health problems, by chanting Daimoku. She impressed me as she really put Buddhist practice focused on the Gohonzon, at the center of her life. One day, we discussed our experiences with chanting Daimoku whilst I was giving her a lift in my car. At the time I had been chanting for some weeks to get a new job, but it had not come about yet. I was growing impatient and I asked her why my wish had yet to be fulfilled. All of a sudden, she had a very serious look on her face and I will never forget the way she said to me: "All wishes of a practitioner of the Lotus Sutra will be fulfilled, sometimes it takes months or years, but there will be an answer!" I asked her what made her so sure about this and who had said that. She told me that Nichiren himself had written this in one of his Gosho. I definitely wanted to read this Gosho.

> Even though one might point at the earth and miss it, or even if the sun might rise in the west, it could never happen that the prayers of a practitioner of the Lotus Sutra would go unanswered. *On Prayer*, WND I: 345

Indeed, in this Gosho, Nichiren assures us of the absolute power of Daimoku to fulfill any prayers. In this sense, he considers Daimoku to be a magnificent *"wish-granting jewel"* fulfilling all desires which a practitioner of the Lotus Sutra might have.

> *Myō* means to be fully endowed, which in turn has the meaning
> of "perfect and full." [...] To illustrate, one drop of the great
> ocean contains within it the waters of all the various rivers that
> flow into the ocean, and a single wish-granting jewel, though
> no bigger than a mustard seed, is capable of showering down
> the treasures that one could wish for with all the wish-granting
> jewels.   *The Daimoku of the Lotus Sutra,* WND I: 146

I have often been deeply astonished about Nichiren's firm conviction as to the wonderful power of Daimoku. As this Gosho
states, one meaning of "myō" is "to be fully endowed" which indicates that whatever you wish to create, already exists. You just
have to open the Treasure Tower and activate the wish-granting
jewel by chanting Daimoku.

> The Gohonzon is a certificate of warrant which
> guarantees the fulfilling of all possible desires.

Working together with cosmic power

At the beginning of my practice, I often wondered whether this
was rather like Aladdin's Magic Lamp. Was this just magic? Are we
hoping for some form of divine intervention which leads to a miracle? Or is it rather that our own power and effort leads to the
fulfilment of our wishes?

In the meantime, I have learned that Nichiren's Buddhist philosophy offers a middle way in the sense that we make a determined
effort (self-power) *and* at the same time we get support from a
higher force other than ourselves (other-power). Mr. Daisaku
Ikeda characterizes this specific feature of Nichiren Buddhist practice as follows:

> The Zen practice of just sitting is representative of the kind of
> *jiriki,* or "self-power," practice that makes no appeal to any kind
> of absolute truth or being beyond oneself. On the other hand,
> the chanting of *nembutsu,* relying on and seeking salvation in

Amida Buddha, is representative of the *tariki*, or "other-power," approach. Drawing upon the teachings of the *Lotus Sutra*, Nichiren declared that it was wiser to avoid leaning too much on either the self-power or the other-power approach. Nichiren's practice of chanting *Nam-myoho-renge-kyo* leads us to discover a power and wisdom that exists within us and at the same time transcends us. It embraces aspects of both the self- and other-power practices.   *From an interview published in the Buddhist magazine Tricycle of Winter 2008.*

You can find this concept in the Gosho summarized below:

[Practicing the Lotus Sutra today includes both aspects of self-power and other-power because one's own life is endowed with the Buddhahood of all beings.]   *The Meaning of the Sacred Teachings of the Buddha's lifetime*, WND II: 62

Whenever we chant, we are connected to something greater than ourselves: that is, to a cosmic consciousness which reacts to our intentions. That's why it is so important to be aware of both: a connection to cosmic consciousness and a clear vision of what we want to achieve.

Such an insight has been accepted by Dr. Dirk Meijer, professor of pharmacology at the university of Groningen in the Netherlands: in one of his papers, he claims that:

Our individual mind should be seen as a part of a larger universal consciousness, which itself is functional within the entire fabric of reality.

This means that if you try to realize your goal just by relying upon your own will, knowledge and effort, you will be overwhelmed by all the challenges you have to confront and you will become exhausted in the end. Yet, on the other hand, if you just rely on the power outside of yourself, you will never develop your own ability and capacity to meet any challenge required for your personal growth. For you need both.

> The practice of chanting Daimoku contains both the aspects of self-power *and* other-power. You decide what you want in life and you take full responsibility for your life while you attain resonance with the universe and gain benevolent support from it. Thus, you always work with that cosmic consciousness which is both inherent and external to yourself in order to realize your wishes.

Clearly, Nichiren was trying to teach us that when we chant, we activate certain functions that are inscribed in the Gohonzon. He also tells us that these functions are like natural laws. In another Gosho, Nichiren tells us that his Buddhist teaching is in accordance with "natural laws or with natural phenomena", as he explains in the following reply to the wife of Shijō Kingo.

> Tiantai states that if a woman's faith is weak, even though she embraces the Lotus Sutra, she will be forsaken. For example, if a commanding general is fainthearted, his soldiers will become cowards. If a bow is weak, the bowstring will be slack. If the wind is gentle, the waves will never rise high. *This all accords with the principles of nature.*
>
> The Unity of Husband and Wife, WND I: 464

In order to understand these functions better, it is helpful to update Nichiren's metaphorical expressions into the contemporary language of science. This will help us to delve more deeply into the wonderful function and power which is inherent to the practice of chanting Daimoku focusing on a Mandala Gohonzon.

Myō-hō-ren-ge-kyō is the foundation of all things

I was really excited and fascinated by Nichiren's unshakable conviction! Yet I wondered as to how could he be so certain about the wish-fulfilling effect of Daimoku? What was the secret of his conviction? Keeping this question in mind, let's take a closer look at what the "Mantra of Nam-myō-hō-ren-ge-kyō" really represents: what it signifies at the deepest level.

First, the "Daimoku of Myōhōrengekyō" literally means the "title of the Lotus Sutra". Traditionally, when the "Daimoku of Nam-Myōhōrengekyō" was recited in the Tendai school in which Nichiren studied, it signified, as the prefix "Nam" suggests, paying homage to the Sutra itself and devoting oneself to its title. Yet frequently I asked myself: `What does it mean to recite the title of a sutra? Is the quintessence of the sutra embodied in this way? Such kinds of literal explanations of the Daimoku confused me for quite a long time, as they simply didn't make sense to me. I believed rather that Nichiren's understanding must have gone far beyond any such literal interpretation of the Daimoku.

Fortunately, I found a clear answer to my question in a Gosho in which Nichiren considered some fundamental questions, such as: why should we only chant Daimoku instead of devoting ourselves to Tiantai's meditation on Ichinen Sanzen?; how could the practice of chanting Daimoku obtain for us enormous benefits even without any knowledge of its meaning? It is characteristic of Nichiren to refer to natural phenomena in explaining the significance of chanting Daimoku.

> When a baby drinks milk, it has no understanding of its taste, and yet its body is naturally nourished. [...]
> When plants and trees receive the rainfall, they can hardly be aware of what they are doing, and yet do they not proceed to put forth blossoms?
> The five characters of Myo-ho-ren-ge-kyo do not represent the sutra text, nor are they its meaning. They are nothing other than the intent of the entire sutra. So, even though beginners in Buddhist practice may not understand their significance, by practicing these five characters, they will naturally conform to the sutra's intent.
> *On the Four Stages of Faith and the Five Stages of Practice*,
> WND I: 788

The Lotus Sutra proclaims a universal message that everyone can attain enlightenment by embracing and upholding the Lotus

Sutra, or its essence, the Mystic Law (*Myōhō*). However, this law of cause and effect as related to enlightenment seemed to me to be overly abstract. The enlightened state of life must be attained in a quite natural way, just as Nichiren always emphasized. Indeed, Nichiren considered this possibility of enlightenment to be fundamentally rooted in "Buddha-nature", the doctrine about which was developed after the Lotus Sutra had been compiled in the 2nd Century AD. Furthermore, Nichiren no longer regarded the Buddha-nature as merely the "quality of an enlightened person", but rather as the foundation of all beings and all things throughout nature and the universe.

> Myoho-renge-kyo is the Buddha-nature of all living beings. The Buddha-nature is the Dharma nature, and the Dharma nature is enlightenment.
> The Buddha-nature possessed by Shakyamuni, Tahō, and [...] — the Buddha-nature that all these beings possess is called by the name Myoho-renge-kyo.
> *Conversation between a Sage and an Unenlightened Man,*
> WND I, p.130

Thus, the universal Buddha-nature considered as the foundation of all things is that which is to be attained through our practice. Consequently, I became firmly convinced by Nichiren's powerful idea that the Daimoku of Nam-Myōhōrengekyō itself is the exclusive "mantra" which alone should be practiced in order to activate the Buddha-nature inherent both within and without our own lives.

With such an understanding, I found that I could now relate to the reason why Nichiren had inscribed this mantra at the center of his Mandala Gohonzon. For it is a clear demonstration that all beings and all things manifest their Buddha-nature through chanting it and that they are thereby all inter-connected on the spiritual dimension.

This is an indication that Nichiren considered the "practice of chanting Daimoku" (*Shōdaigyō*) as central to his practice, while the recitation of the sutra itself should be considered only to be an auxiliary practice. By these means, Nichiren established an extraordinarily innovative form of Buddhist practice which is nevertheless firmly built upon the tradition of the Lotus Sutra:

"Myohorengekyo" literally refers to the title of the Lotus Sutra, but in the context of Nichiren Buddhist practice, it signifies the universal Buddha-nature which is the foundation and the source of all things in the universe. Chanting the mantra of Nam-Myōhōrengekyō enables us to activate the Buddha-nature inherent in our own lives and thereby to transform all suffering into happiness.

Thus, Nichiren considered the mantra of Nam-myō-hō-ren-ge-kyō to be the essential means of attaining to enlightenment itself. Yet I also began to ask myself: what in fact is "en-lighten-ment"? Does it have something to do with "light"? Well, we will see.

Rendering Buddhist concepts into a modern terminology

Toda's theory of life

Josei Toda (1900-1958) explained that the traditional terms "Buddha" or "Buddha nature" mean "life." When we die, however, he believed that each individual life returns to the universe and is dissolved into the great ocean of cosmic life. Toda regarded this cosmic life as an inherent part of our physical world and shared the view that life is actually omnipresent in all things. It is non-local, transcendent, and eternal; it is the essence of the universe from which all things originate and emerge and to which all things return. He was the first person to render the traditional Buddhist term "Buddha nature" into a truly modern interpretation:

> The Buddha means life, the cosmic life that is inherent in my life as well as in the universe. It is the essence of the universe itself.

Correspondingly Toda also regarded the Gohonzon as an embodiment of this cosmic life principle and called it a "happiness-producing machine." In this way, he encouraged people to believe in the power of the Gohonzon and to put its miraculous mechanism into action. Thus, he inspired hundreds of thousands of people in Japan, in the postwar period, to overcome poverty, illness and conflicts in their families and social lives.

Life is light

Nowadays, Toda's modern view of "cosmic life" as the essence of the universe, can be further refined if we look at several research developments which define "life" in a more definite way. One such approach is that of the late German biophysicist Dr. Fritz Albert Popp (1939 - 2018), who defined "life" essentially as "light". We all need light in order to feel happy. You feel much better when you feel the energy of sunlight on your skin, don't you? Sunshine is essential for all living beings in order to thrive and to grow. However, did you know that it is not just the sun that radiates light, but all living beings are likewise radiating light at the organic cellular and bodily level? This light consists of biophotons.

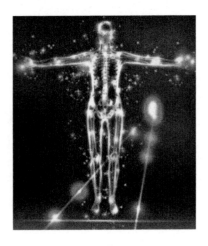

The phenomenon of "biophoton emission" was first discovered in the 1920s in Russia, but later empirically verified by Popp in the 1970s.

Light seems to be the life force your cells communicate with.

His research demonstrates that there is light radiating from each of our cells. Every living being, each plant, animal and human cell, radiates coherent, well-ordered, regularly patterned light in the form of biophotons. The biophotons from all of the cells in your body together form the bioenergetic field around you.

What exactly is a photon?

A photon is the smallest physical unit of light that is a carrier of information and energy. It always transports or conveys the same amount of energy with the speed of light, regardless of distance. What does it mean for a photon to move at the speed of light? What does it look like? Well, a pho-

ton has no mass and travels at the constant speed of light of about 300,000 kilometers per second. It could travel around the earth 7.5 times in one second. Just imagine! This is an amazing speed which actually makes the photon a perfect energy provider.

But there is something else which photons are known for: a photon is a quantum. In physics, a quantum is the smallest unit of a physical property like energy or matter. In other words, the photon is one of the smallest particles in the quantum world. Furthermore, there is something really astonishing about it: it has a dual nature and can behave like a particle and a wave at the same time.

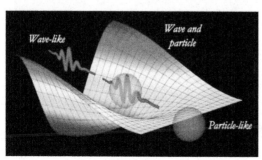

It can be energy *and* matter at the same time. So, think of the photon as the threshold between energy and matter.

A photon can behave like a wave
and a particle

For this reason, a photon produces an electric and a magnetic vibration at the same time forming an electromagnetic field. Once photons form an electromagnetic field, they are in their wave state, which means they are in their energy state.

Electromagnetic Wave

Light is an electromagnetic wave

The energy field around our body

Photons also form the electromagnetic energy field around our body. When we talk about our energy patterns, we mean the arrangement of photons within our biofield.

Thus, managing our energy means changing the photon arrangement within our energy field. Our body becomes a reflection of the photon arrangements in our energy field.

Professor Meijer described this phenomenon in one of his papers on consciousness referring to our body being in resonance with the "zero-point field". The zero-point energy field has often been

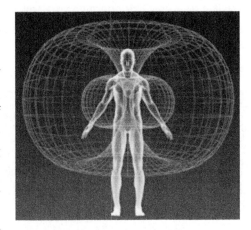

Human electro-magnetic field around the body

associated with an eternal and unchanging unified field of consciousness underlying everything and permeating the whole of
creation:

> Photon-like waves are permanently present in our body
> through resonance, as the organism is embedded in the zero-
> point energy field.

What does this mean for our practice of chanting Daimoku? Our
measurements have demonstrated that when we chant Daimoku,
we increase our biophoton emissions and the electromagnetic
field around our body. That's when we are more energy than matter.

As such, there is no time or space difference between us and
another person. This explains the non-local quantum effect of Daimoku. You can affect another person by chanting Daimoku without having to be physically with that person or in the same space.
This can only happen in a quantum universe. Nichiren put it this
way:

> There is in the entire world no place where the sound of chant-
> ing Daimoku can't reach.
> From *Nikō's Records of Nichiren's lectures
> on the Lotus Sutra* held at Minobu between 1278 and 1280

This is especially interesting and important because our intentions also generate electromagnetic fields as we shall see later on.
I wondered also whether photons were a perfect energy provider
for our intentions and visions? Could they make our intentions coherent and laser-like? This is just another way of saying that they
are extremely powerful.

Health and communication require coherence

Another question is: What do photons actually do in our bodies?
Researchers have found that the biophotons in our bodies are the
conveyors of information and serve as a means of communication

both between cells and within cells. In other words, our cells communicate with each other via light. This light tells every cell what to do. Popp stated that coherent light controls every metabolic process in our body. It is our life force which powers our body. This life force consists of photons.

Popp considered biophotons to be carriers of information both within our body and towards the quantum field. Information can only be conveyed if the light is coherent, meaning that there is no disorder or blockage which might cause disturbances in the transmission of information.

Furthermore, Popp discovered that healthy organisms have coherent light. When we get ill and suffer from a disease, this light becomes weak and incoherent; not in phase; not aligned. Without the natural flow of information, communication and order, your cells and their surrounding tissue will become disordered or incoherent which according to Popp, is the starting point for any illness.

There is an "information blockage" in your cells and the surrounding tissue becomes ill. A more powerful way of understanding a blockage is to imagine it as an absence of vital life force. Biophotons are nothing other than vital life energy. And where energy isn´t flowing, there is a point in your body where the movement of life force is blocked. The result is that this point falls into a state of disorder or incoherence.

According to Professor Meijer from the university of Groningen in the Netherlands referred to above, such a state of disorder or incoherence leads to a gradual loss of cellular organization which results in illnesses such as cancer.

As it is precisely this more ordered state which allows information to flow freely between and within the cells of our body, any incoherent, disordered state - prevents information flowing freely (see picture 1).

Information is only freely and efficiently transmitted in a coherent, orderly state where the cells are in a coherent state, not blocking free flow (see picture 2).

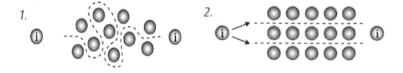

We know today that the degree of coherence of the energy field
around our body reveals the state of our health.

Our life energy and light

Today, Popp´s findings are well established in the international scientific world. Research on biophoton energy is being carried out worldwide. At first, he was fiercely attacked for his discoveries in 1980s Germany and he eventually lost his professorship. That´s because he introduced a vitalistic concept of life energy that went against the materialist and mechanistic worldview of traditional science. For, traditional science considers the human body to be like a machine that is only run by chemical and material processes. The research on biophotons, however, suggests something different:

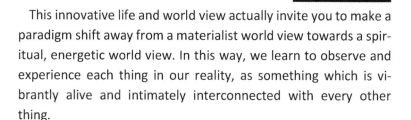

There is a life force within us
that is related to light.

This innovative life and world view actually invite you to make a paradigm shift away from a materialist world view towards a spiritual, energetic world view. In this way, we learn to observe and experience each thing in our reality, as something which is vibrantly alive and intimately interconnected with every other thing.

The world we live in is full of life and energy!

Such an understanding of the world as vibrating with energy and life, accords with the concept of "life energy" such as that denoted by the term "Prana" in India, "Qi" in China and "Ki" in Japan; a concept which underlies all of life's processes. That is why Josei Toda's understanding of the term "buddha" in terms of "life" or "life force," offered a profound insight into our everyday experience.

It is this seemingly magical power that life represents for us. It can also be called life energy. We usually only appreciate it when we no longer possess it: When we feel weak, tired or no longer able to perform. It often has nothing to do with age. There are children who have completely lost their vitality and there are 80-year old whose batteries are still completely full. But without energy, life becomes torture. If you feel 20 years younger than you are, it means that you have enough life energy. But if you constantly feel tired or older than you are, then it is time to fill up your batteries. Some researchers have tried to measure this life energy in a kinesiological way. The results have shown that when you have 100% of your life energy, you basically feel like you are flying, and life seems to be easy to handle. When you have 80% of your life energy, you are fully efficient, and you achieve your goals. If you have 70% of it, you just feel normal, but you know that you have experienced better times before.

If you have 50%, you will still hold on, but everything is no longer fun. If you have only 30% life energy, you will be exhausted after only 2 hours of work and you will only drag yourself through life. If you have 20% life energy left, your battery is basically empty. Our measurements have shown that chanting Daimoku is a very efficient way to enhance and strengthen the energy field around your body and to fill up your energy level.

Exercise

What do you think: how high is your life energy in general at the moment?

_____

How much life energy do you currently have between 0 and 100%? My life energy is _____%.

When you chant Daimoku – how do you feel? Can you feel an increase in your life energy after 30 minutes of Daimoku?

_____

After 30 minutes of Daimoku I feel an increase in my life energy of _____%?

Chapter 4
Light is the foundation of Life

We know today that man, essentially, is a being of light.
– Fritz Albert Popp

Communicating with light

As referred to above, through measurement we know that chanting Daimoku enhances the energy field around your body by increasing the biophoton emissions of your body. This means we are emitting more light when we are chanting.

Thus, if we are told that we activate our "enlightened" being while chanting Daimoku, this may be true in the most literal sense.

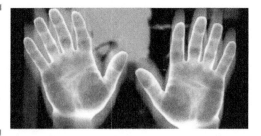

We exist far beyond our physical self. We are far more than the atoms and molecules that make up our bodies; rather, we are beings of light. Biophotons are emitted by the human body. According to Dr. Gary Schwartz of the University of Arizona, they are emitted by all mental activity and especially when we send a healing intention to someone. Furthermore, they modulate the fundamental processes and communication within and between our cells and DNA.

Biophotons are emitted by all mental activity.

This means that our visions and intentions are made of the very life force that runs through our body; that which we activate when we chant Daimoku. Daimoku seems to be the bearer and enhancer of our intentions and visions. This also suggests that the energy we create when chanting Daimoku is the source of the energy of our visions and intentions.

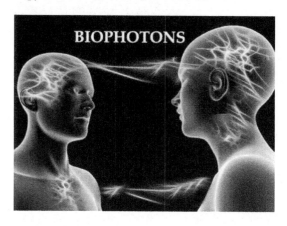

We also seem to communicate with each other via the photons of the electromagnetic fields which surround each of us. Professor Meijer believes that we not only communicate with each other via words, but that we also send subliminal messages to each other at the energetic level via such electromagnetic fields. He came to this conclusion because brain scanning studies from recent years demonstrate that when two people talk to each other, the EEG patterns exhibited by their brains are soon seen to correlate with each other, almost as if they are one person. This indicates that there is a type of connection between them which relies on extremely rapid photon transmission, generated by their electromagnetic fields. Without saying anything, we can communicate that which is in our mind. We are transmitting visions and intentions.

That's why it is important to have a clear vision and intention. If the energy of our own visions and intentions is unfocused and weak, we simply become a magnet for all kinds of other energies, we just draw in load of totally random energies and the electromagnetic field around us becomes overwhelmed by the ocean of energy vibrations which surround us. That's when other people are running your life.

Biophotons are also emitted by plants. Dr. Schwartz has been using an imaging system to look at biophotons with a CCD camera. This device can record the very faint light from outer space and detect ongoing patterns of high frequency radiation, such as cosmic rays. Thus, he has also been able to photograph light coming from leaves.

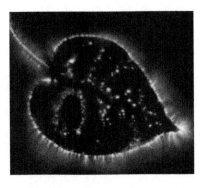

Light being emitted by a leaf

He has also demonstrated that the light which a person emits, increases when they are projecting their intention to someone else, e.g. in cases of intentional healing. Light would appear to play a vital role in the healing process. Light is the foundation of all life, states Dr. Popp. Interestingly, this is exactly what Nichiren taught us about Nam-Myoho-Renge-Kyo.

The Buddhism of the sun

Do you happen to know the reason why Nichiren gave himself the name "Nichi-Ren" which means Sun-Lotus? The Sino-Japanese character "Nichi" stands for "sun" and highlights the beneficial function of the sun in illuminating the darkness of ignorance of all people and the world.

> As the light of the sun and moon can dispel all opacity and gloom so this person as he advances through the world can illuminate the darkness of all living beings. *LS, Chapter 21:* 318.

Nichiren attributed this illuminating character of light also to the effect of chanting Daimoku in lighting up the dark and transforming any suffering we are exposed to. He tells us that chanting

Daimoku is the light which illuminates our life and transforms our suffering:

> Today, when Nichiren and his followers recite [the mantra of] Nam-myō-hō-ren-ge-kyō, they are illuminating the darkness of birth and death, making it clear, so that the wisdom fire of nirvana may shine forth.
>
> *OTT*: 10

Daimoku is radiating light energy

As this Gosho shows, Nichiren consistently equated the beneficial effects of chanting Daimoku to the emission of light. Thus, whenever we chant, we radiate a powerful light not only within our body but also from our body towards the entire world.

I was fascinated by this wonderful idea. Yet how would Nichiren represent this radiant, light emitting character of Daimoku? In fact, he evoked an image of this luminous energy field by the particular way in which he inscribed the characters of Nam-myō-hō-ren-ge-kyō at the center of his Mandala Gohonzon. Thus inscribed, the Daimoku is radiant with light. Nichiren Buddhist scholars refer to the stylistic "points of light" or the "light emitting points" (*kōmyōten*) with which Nichiren further adorned the mantra he had inscribed at the center of the Gohonzon. These points of light most emphatically portray the characters of the Daimoku as each emitting vibrant rays of light, as explained below.

As an example, let's look at the Gohonzon he inscribed in March 1280 at Mount Minobu. If he had simply used the standard characters to inscribe the mantra, the seven Chinese characters would have looked

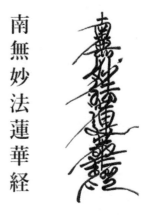

Pic. A   Pic. B

as in picture A. But Nichiren actually inscribed the mantra of *Nam-myō-hō-ren-ge-kyō* as in picture B.

If we compare the standard form of characters with Nichiren's bold adornment of the mantra, we immediately notice that Nichiren's unique handwritten characters are vigorously extended in a particularly dynamic manner.

This calligraphic adornment of "points of light" to the central Daimoku is a stylistic motif adopted by Nichiren's successors up to the present day.

Nichiren scholars agree that these vigorously extended strokes emphasize Nichiren's determined intention and great compassion to represent and to spread the vibrant light energy of Daimoku in order to illuminate the darkness in our lives and throughout the whole world.

In practical terms, Nichiren teaches us that the light of Daimoku has the power to raise up and to illuminate all the other states of life and being which are inscribed on the Gohonzon. This is vigorously affirmed by the light emitting power of the Daimoku at the center of the Gohonzon.

Nichiren explained the meaning of the Mandala Gohonzon and the particular significance of the centrally placed Daimoku radiating light energy as follows.

> [All the Ten Worlds of Buddhas, bodhisattva ...] dwell in this Gohonzon. Illuminated by the light of the five characters of the Mystic Law, they display the dignified natures which they inherently possess. This is called the object of devotion.
>
> *The Real Aspect of the Gohonzon*
> *(Reply to the lady Nichinyo),* WND I: 832

The light emitting function of chanting Daimoku is the ultimate source from which we develop our highest potential and transform all the negative aspects of our life into positive aspects.

Consciousness is light and energy

Nichiren consistently used the image of light when describing the effects of chanting Daimoku, which he specifically referred to as "the light that illuminates the darkness". Today we know that this is literally the case. Through measurement, we know that chanting Daimoku enhances the energy field around our body by increasing biophoton emissions. This means we are actually emitting more light when chanting. That´s when I realized that "enlightenment" really is quite literally "light".

When we activate our enlightened state of life through chanting Daimoku we increase biophoton emissions in our body that quite literally begins to shine.

According to German biophysicist Dr. Michael König, our state of consciousness depends on the strength of the biophoton field around our body. He claims that the biophoton field around our body is directly related to our state of consciousness and to our state of life. He considers that consciousness and energy are intimately interrelated and cannot be divided. He states that pure consciousness consists of photons. This means it is fundamentally light.

Thus, we now have a novel understanding of the concept of "Buddha nature" as equivalent to "cosmic life" which is inherently related to pure cosmic consciousness and to light or photons.

Experiencing cosmic consciousness

Some people attain this level of consciousness as a result of having a near-death experience. In our book "Nichiren Buddhism 3.0," we described the amazing experiences of Anita Moorjani who overcame cancer while being in a coma. In our book "Nichiren

Buddhism 3.1," we also described the fascinating experience of Dr. Eben Alexander, a Harvard trained neurosurgeon, who had fallen into a coma due to an acute bacterial inflammation of the brain. The neurological functions of his brain deteriorated rapidly, and he was given a 90 percent chance of dying. In the subsequent coma which lasted seven days, he experienced a completely different dimension of non-local consciousness, far beyond ordinary, local, everyday consciousness.

Dr. Alexander had previously been a proponent of the materialist view, that consciousness is just a by-product of the brain. After having experienced a radically different dimension of consciousness, he began to speak about this. As he explained in his speech to the Theosophical society: "This was not the consciousness of Eben Alexander, this was the consciousness we all share, far more powerful – a direct link to the divine". At this level he felt a deep and unconditional love and directly experienced what he describes as "that infinite all loving creative power far beyond any naming". Whilst in this state, he received the reassurance that "we are always loved and cherished" and that "we will be taken care of".

We are always loved and cherished, and we will be taken care of.

He also realized that "we cannot do any wrong" as long as we are aware that we "reap what we sow". This means that we either experience the feelings we have evoked in other people directly here in this life or as a kind of "review" after we have died. Whatever you have caused another person to feel, you yourself will feel at some point. So, Dr. Alexander was aware of the principle of cause and effect which is one of the functions of cosmic consciousness.

He experienced a profound realization that we are all eternal spiritual beings transmigrating through multiple incarnations and that we all have lessons to learn to do with love. But most importantly, he considered the reality of non-local consciousness to be far more real than the everyday reality of our three-dimensional world. He lost his fear of death because he knows from direct experience that we are truly at home in the spiritual realm. Compared to the reality he experienced when close to death, he considers this world to be no more than a "dream": for him, non-local consciousness is "more real". Interestingly, this is exactly what Nichiren stated when he suggested that ordinary people are in a dream-like state.

> The Buddha is like a person awake and ordinary people are like persons dreaming. Therefore when the people wake from their empty dreams of birth and death and return to their waking state of original enlightenment, they will experience the state of instant enlightenment and enjoy the great wisdom of equality and the Law that does not make any distinctions.
>
> *The Unanimous Declaration by the Buddhas*, WND II: 841

In this Gosho, Nichiren teaches us that at the level of cosmic consciousness, there are no distinctions. From the perspective of the awakened state, all distinctions such as birth and death, good and bad, right and left, north and south, past and future, male and female and so on, are all fabricated by our deluded mind in a state of dreaming. Any distinction causes us to differentiate ourselves from other people and other things which can lead inexorably to discrimination and segregation. At the level of cosmic consciousness, however, all these distinctions do not ultimately exist. Everyone is equal and is part of the unity of consciousness. We are all one.

Eben Alexander considers that we do not need a near-death experience to access this level, for he was able to revisit the experiences he had had near to death, through prayer and deep meditation. According to Nichiren, we can most swiftly access this level by simply chanting Daimoku before the Gohonzon.

Speaking of this level of consciousness deep within our own lives, Nichiren referred to it as the 9th consciousness. This deepest level of our subconsciousness is real and relates to a certain mechanism which we can activate every time we chant Daimoku before the Gohonzon.

Myoho-renge-kyo represents cosmic consciousness which is the foundation of the universe and is always present like the reverse side of a coin. It is eternal and indestructible.

What Nichiren taught in the above Gosho is that fundamentally, reality is not just the world of material, physical forms perceived by our senses. For the physical world is a manifestation of consciousness. Consciousness is primary. Ultimately, there is only consciousness which is expressing itself in diverse forms and experiences. And the source of all these forms and experiences is pure, enlightened consciousness.

If everything derives from the level of consciousness,
it is only logical that this is the level we must begin with
if we want to change our life.

Exercise

Are you aware of an increase of life energy while chanting Daimoku?

_ _

Do you feel that you are somehow connected to people you love, as well as to nature and the universe more widely?

_ _

Chapter 5
The fascinating design of the Mandala

In resonance with pure consciousness

Let's return to the miracle mechanism inscribed on the Gohonzon. Initially, we asked the question as to why Nichiren was so convinced about the wish-fulfilling effect of Daimoku. Keeping this question in mind: let's take a closer look at what the "mantra of Nam-myō-hō-ren-ge-kyō" actually represents and what it means at the deepest level.

Whenever we chant this mantra, we activate the functions which are represented on the Gohonzon, that is primarily the function of transformation and the additional protective and supportive functions. We will be guided. We can transform our emotional and physical pain and we will be supported in achieving our goals. Yet the most important function is that which both transforms our state of life and increases our energy. But how is this possible? How can we actually transform our state of life by chanting the mantra of Nam-myō-hō-ren-ge-kyō before the Gohonzon? Well, as noted earlier above, we have recorded an increase in biophoton emissions while chanting Daimoku to the Gohonzon. So that's when the biophoton field around our body increases.

According to Dr. Michael König, we dramatically increase our energy level when the biophoton field around our body becomes resonant with the photons of pure consciousness. Dr. König claims also that it is this resonance between our own biophoton field and this universal high-energy photon field which elevates our own energy.

By putting our own biophoton field into resonance with photons of pure consciousness, we can elevate our own state of life.

It is a fascinating phenomenon when we are in resonance with the universal field of cosmic consciousness. We then find ourselves in synchronicity with everyone else who is resonant with this field. Immediately, we attract people who protect us or support us or are simply just good for us. When we align with this field, our individual minds automatically synchronize with every other mind which is likewise synchronized with this field.

We should imagine it like this: If there are two guitars at opposite ends of a room which are tuned to each other and the G string of one of the guitars is plucked, the G string on the other guitar will also vibrate. The same dynamic occurs between human beings. The more we are in resonance with pure consciousness, the more we are in tune with those who are likewise resonant with cosmic consciousness.

And this is exactly what Nichiren said. He described this phenomenon of resonance between our individual minds and the universal mind while chanting Daimoku in one of his Gosho. In order to explain the miracle effect of the recitation of this mantra, he provided a beautiful metaphor of this resonance by referring to birds singing together as a chorus in unison.

The Buddha nature that all these beings possess is called by the name Myoho-renge-kyo. Therefore, if you recite this [mantra] once, then the Buddha nature of all living beings will be summoned and gather around you. At that time the three bodies of the Dharma nature within you—the Dharma body, the reward body, and the manifested body—will be drawn forth and become manifest. This is called realizing the state of Buddha.

To illustrate, when a caged bird sings, the many birds flying in the

> sky all gather around it at once; seeing this, the bird in the cage
> strives to get out.   *A Sage and an unenlightened Man*,
>   WND I: 131

Consequently, the Daimoku at the center of the Gohonzon suggests that the primary means of manifesting an enlightened state of life is simply by chanting this particular mantra before the Gohonzon. Observing the Mandala, we become vividly aware that each of the representatives of the ten worlds which represent the ten life states of life such as the Buddhas, the Bodhisattvas and all the other representatives, including all the deities and demons, are each chanting the mantra of Nam-myō-hō-ren-ge-kyō. By so doing, each manifests their enlightened state of life, resonant with Nam-myō-hō-ren-ge-kyō. Even the negative energies of the universe, represented by the demons, thereby manifest the highest state of life and can thereby be transformed into positive energies that support us.

Thus, the wondrous design of the Mandala Gohonzon and the chanting of Daimoku while focusing on it, enables us to activate the miracle mechanism of becoming resonant with universal pure consciousness, the means whereby we can enjoy those wonderful experiences which exceed our everyday reality and expectations.

That's when the whole cosmos has our back. That's when we can achieve things which we could never achieve from our own individual resources or by means of our own distinct, separate identity; through relying solely on our own ego-consciousness. The more connected we are to this energy-field of the spirit, the more miraculous our lives become. Our suffering diminishes. For the primary cause of human suffering and pain, as Deepak Chopra put it, is separation from this energy-field of life when we are not tuned into universal consciousness

Thus, each time we chant to the Gohonzon, we activate
the essence and source of the whole cosmos itself,
and become connected to the cosmic field of consciousness.

Gohonzon first

The syllable "nam" indicates that you are devoting yourself to the source of all phenomena; to cosmic consciousness, the Mystic Law which is permanently manifesting and governing everything that happens, not only in our own lives, but also throughout the entire universe. We are opening ourselves to cosmic intelligence.

Thus, by chanting "nam"-myoho-renge-kyo, you are basically expressing your sense of deep trust. What you are basically saying is: "I don't want my coffee yet, I don't want any distraction, I don't want any trivial comfort. I don't want my cell phone, my emails, all I want is the direct connection to you, the divine intelligence within me! You are the object of my entire attention and affection, my whole passion and ultimate devotion. And I am going to invest all my attention and trust in you as you are the source of my absolute happiness. I am going to make contact with you every single day!"

And as we begin to make contact with this energy-field of pure consciousness while chanting, we will embody its life force and vibrant energy as we interact with it. That's when we begin to experience more wholeness, more coherence in our brains. We have measured it. Equally, e develop a brighter and more coherent energy field around our bodies. We have measured this as well!

Now we can access this energy and take it back to our own lives and thereby realize our hopes and visions. With this fundamental connection to the field of cosmic consciousness, we can enjoy our coffee and enjoy our whole new state of being!

Nichiren believed that it was essential for us to devote ourselves to the deepest foundation of our lives. He was especially firm in this regard. He considered that the highest priority in our lives should be to devote ourselves to the practice of Daimoku.

> Since nothing is more precious than life itself, one who dedicates one's life to Buddhist practice is certain to attain Buddhahood. [...]
>
> The way of the world dictates that one should repay a great obligation to another, even at the cost of one's life. Many warriors die for their lords, perhaps many more than one would imagine. A man will die to defend his honor; a woman will die for a man.
>
> Fishes want to survive in a pond and dig holes deeper into the bottom to hide while deploring its shallowness. Yet tricked by bait, they take the hook. Birds are afraid of sitting too low on the tree and perch on the higher branches. But they are lured by bait and go into the net.
>
> Human beings are equally vulnerable. They give their lives for all kinds of superficial worldly matters but rarely for the Buddha's precious teachings. No wonder none of them attains Buddhahood.   *Letter from Sado*, WND I: 301

The miracle mechanism found within the Mandala

I have always been fascinated by Nichiren's mandala. I consider it the most beautiful and awesome creation on earth. I was even more impressed by its general design when I began to understand something of the principles behind its construction and the meaning embedded deep within it. Though there are many fascinating aspects to speak of in this respect, let's just take a look at the fundamental aspects which determine the operation of the miracle mechanism activated by chanting Daimoku. This should enable us to understand why Nichiren was so deeply convinced that no prayer of a practitioner of the Lotus Sutra would go unanswered.

We find the answer in the Mandala Gohonzon itself which Nichiren especially created to be a unique object of meditative focus and devotion. When we observe the Gohonzon we immediately become aware of several extraordinarily bold characters at its center and at each of its four corners. We also become aware of two enormous Sanskrit characters inscribed on the right and left in the middle of the Gohonzon. As I can't read or understand those characters, I asked my husband Yukio to illustrate their meaning through their traditional iconographic forms. He provided me with the image below.

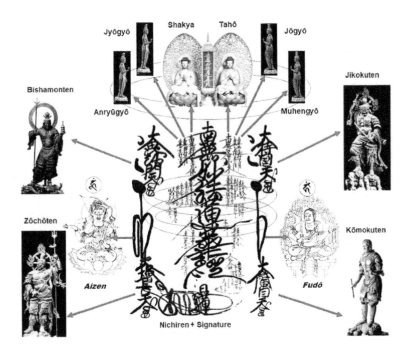

This illustration highlights the fundamental structure of the Mandala Gohonzon. For greater clarity, almost all the representatives of the Ten Worlds have been omitted on this image. Only the two Buddhas and the Four Bodhisattvas of the Earth found at the highest level of the Mandala have been included.

To fuse with the Gohonzon

As explained above, as soon as we chant the mantra of "Nam-myō-hō-ren-ge-kyō", we begin to activate the Mystic Law as depicted at the center of the Mandala Gohonzon. While chanting, we begin to manifest the enlightened state of life within ourselves. You might ask yourself whether we are actually enlightened while we chant Daimoku? What does it mean to be enlightened? What does it feel like?

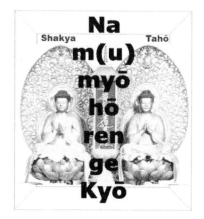

In actuality, this question is answered by *"the two Buddhas, Shakyamuni and* Tahō, *sitting side by side in the Treasure Tower"*. For they symbolically express the principle traditionally known as "the fusion of subjective wisdom with objective reality" (*kyōchimyōgō*). To put it in a more practical way, this means we are fused with the boundless universe itself. We begin to feel a connection to everyone, to everything, and to every time and place and our sense of separation between ourselves and our envisioned futures begins to dissolve.

> The two Buddhas represent the enlightened state of life
> and the fusion with pure and unlimited cosmic consciousness.
> In this state of life all possibilities of abundant
> wisdom and happiness become available.

This mechanism which is built into the Mandala, is activated whenever we chant Daimoku, especially if we absolutely identify ourselves with this "object of devotion" and actually become one with it. What this means is that we chant Daimoku in such a focused way that we have only "one thought or intention" (*Ichinen*) to become at one with the Gohonzon. This cannot be attained by focusing in an aggressive highly stressed manner, but only if we rather relax and let go of all our daily concerns and anxieties. All that is required is a simple trust while chanting Daimoku to the Gohonzon.

Once we are so completely absorbed in the act of chanting itself then we are in a flowing state. We forget ourselves. We forget time and we even forget our environment. For it is not our own ego which is chanting, but rather something far greater is active throughout this process. We should be aware of our hearts while chanting to the Gohonzon, noticing the feeling of joy and compassion emerging from deep within our bodies. We are here and now, completely tuned into to the present moment.

The Mandala Gohonzon serves as a clear mirror
for us to observe our hearts, our enlightened state of life.

In this spiritual state, we are Bodhisattvas of the Earth who in essence are enlightened persons. At that moment, as Nichiren imaginatively puts it, we are within the Gohonzon while at the same time, the Gohonzon is within us! It could be said as well that we are embedded in the vast ocean of life force energy which surrounds us and which at the same time, is also within us. That's when our local, particular, individual consciousness merges with the non-local, universal, cosmic consciousness. We feel an increase in the physical energy of our bodies and experience a clear luminosity of a mind which has completely calmed and settled.

When we are being at one with the Gohonzon,
that's when we are a Buddha!

Chapter 6
The power of transformation

Dissolving energy blockages

After I had finally understood how to chant Daimoku to the Gohonzon, I wondered what an enlightened state of life actually looks and feels like. I asked myself how I might experience its effects. There was a particular aspect which struck me the most. Whenever we activate the miracle mechanism inherent in the Gohonzon, the aspect of transformation is at once apparent. When we chant Daimoku, we can transform our particular circumstances in a general sense. Whatever we feel to be negative and poisonous initially, can be turned into "medicine" through the transformative power of Daimoku. Yet there are even more specific transformative powers inscribed on the Gohonzon. These have the power to transform emotional and physical pain.

According to Dr. Michael König, physical pain is caused by a build-up of electromagnetic energy of biophotons which are then unable to move freely and lead to blockage. Allowing this pent-up energy to flow freely by dissolving blockages, is in fact "transformation." He claims that there are energy blocks which inhibit our direct access to pure consciousness. Unconsciously, we repress many feelings and much emotional pain in our body. In order to eliminate this pain, we require a higher concentration of biophotons to attain a higher state of consciousness. For unpleasant experiences result in a situation in which the concentration of biophotons in our body is depleted, according to Dr. König.

Traumatic experiences, stress, unresolved emotions, disappointment, anxiety and fear result in blockages and disturbances to the free flow of energy throughout our body's biophoton field. Our biophoton field loses coherence and harmony and becomes disordered. This results in a loss of life energy and a reduced bio-photon emission intensity. Consequently, our capacities and our contentment with life decrease while we also become more susceptible to illness.

To illustrate the difference in terms of energy flow, let me once again refer to the GDV measurement results found in our previous book, Nichiren Buddhism 3.0. The picture on the left suggests blockages and disturbances in the energy field, indicating a lack of biophotons where you can see the red arrows. Yet after ten minutes of Daimoku, as shown on the right, the energy flow is restored, the concentration of biophotons has increased.

> We now know that the vitality and quality of life depends on the amount and quality of photons in our body.
>
> *– Lynne McTaggart*

We need an increase in biophotons in order to convert disharmonic photon fields into more harmonic, ordered and coherent photon fields. And that's exactly what transformation is, states Dr. König.

Transformation is the conversion of disharmonic photon fields into harmonic photon fields.

In fact, our measurements have demonstrated that this is exactly what happens when we recite Daimoku to the Gohonzon, as we thereby emit more biophotons and the energy field of our body becomes more coherent. And this principle of transformation is inscribed on the Gohonzon in the form of two vibrant representations. Let´s take a closer look at them.

Transform your grief and pain with Fudo and Aizen

When the enlightened state of life is activated, it functions by means of the two transformative principles represented by *Fudō* and *Aizen* on the Gohonzon. For Nichiren these are the two transformative energies which we activate whenever we chant to the Gohonzon. By so doing, we can transform our grief and pain. Traditionally, they have been iconographically depicted in the form of a terrifying, wrathful warrior who subdues the disobedient and who drives away evil spirits. Such iconography dramatically emphasizes the extraordinary energy which is the essence of these radically transformative powers.

On the Gohonzon, they are found on the middle of the left hand side (*Aizen*) and on the middle of the right hand side (*Fudō*), each represented by a single Sanskrit letter placed between each of two of the heavenly kings.

After some time, I finally realized that having a desire or intention to "chant for" is not at all about getting something new like a car, a house, a job or a change of relationship. It is ultimately about how we feel inside, whether we are free from emotional and physical pain. Otherwise we could never enjoy a new house, a new job or a new relationship. This also implies a change to our karma, for we always suffer according to a particular pattern. I felt deeply the priceless value of having a Gohonzon when my favorite aunt had died. I simply spent the whole day before the Gohonzon. All the money in the world cannot transform our emotional pain. We just cannot enjoy our house or our car when we are depressed or when we suffer from physical pain. That's why it is so important that any vision or intention we might have focuses upon the transformative powers of Fudo and Aizen inscribed on the Gohonzon.

Transforming physical pain

Fudō represents the principle of "transforming the sufferings of birth and death into nirvana" (*Shōji-soku-nehan*). I often asked myself what it actually means to "transform suffering into nirvana"? What does "nirvana" here actually mean? The sufferings of birth and death are the physical suffering of our local, individual existence. The physical pain we must endure when born, when we are ill, when we get old and when we die. No one can escape these sufferings and consequently Nichiren considered the transformative power of Fudō to be essential.

I should admit that I had always viewed the figure of Fudō in a wholly abstract way. I knew about him from my Buddhist studies

at university, as he is a figure universally revered in Buddhism and in Sanskrit he is known as "Achala". He has played an important role in Buddhism in general, as he is portrayed as an esoteric deity who has the power to fight devilish functions which means to over-come obstacles and malign circumstances which are a hindrance to our Buddhist practice. That's why the name Fudō also means "the immovable" because he never bends before any obstacle.

Only once in Japan did it occur to me that for Nichiren, Fudō is an actual transformative power which exists not only in theory, or as a metaphor in a buddhological sense, but actually in the form of a dynamic force and energy, which has the capacity to trans-form our physical pain and suffering.

One evening in Japan I watched a series on TV about a medieval Samurai clan. I vividly remember a scene where one of the Samu-rai fervently prayed to the figure of Fudō asking his help to allevi-ate the pain of illness. That's when I realized that I had not grown up with the belief in Fudō as being an actual power and that for Nichiren and many Japanese, his power was just as real as the power of Maria or Jesus felt by many Christian believers.

I understood that Nichiren himself had a very deep relationship to both Fudō and Aizen from a very early age. In fact, Nichiren had had a vision of both deities where he believed that they had trans-ferred their power to him personally.

We all have to endure the pain of being born, when we are ill, when we age and when we die. As I have said before, I have fre-quently asked myself what it actually means to transform our physical pain (the sufferings of birth and death) into nirvana? What does it mean for my everyday life when I am afflicted by physical pain?

The realm of Nirvana should be understood as a realm of pure consciousness free from pain and suffering. So whenever you con-nect to pure consciousness while chanting, you can transform and overcome all physical pain and suffering.

Enhancing the immune system

How important this is became obvious to me all at once at the beginning of this year 2020. We had heard about the devastating effects of the Corona Virus in China and everybody was anxious that it would soon spread to other countries. However, I assumed that this would pass away in a couple of weeks rather like Swine Flu had in 2009. Yet little did I know that within four weeks the whole world would come to a standstill. It felt unreal. It was frightening to watch the news and to hear about so many people dying all over the world. I often had the feeling that I was a character in a bad science fiction movie.

We had visited Northern Italy only the year before and we had spent a wonderful time in Bergamo, Verona, Parma and Turin with engaging and charming people who had read our books and who had invited us out for stimulating and uplifting evenings. Yet now, the whole region around Bergamo and Turin was the major hot spot in the whole Corona crisis and thousands of people were dying. It was so tragic. And this was happening not only there, but worldwide.

The only thing we could do now was to be careful and to seek to enhance our immune systems. Fortunately, we knew that we had a powerful means to achieve this. For quite coincidently, only a couple of months before, we had carried out research to establish whether chanting Daimoku had a beneficial effect on our immune systems.

I knew that there were studies on the effect that meditation had on our immune systems, where meditators had been tested before and after meditation workshops. The data indicated that meditation of five hours a day over a period of four days, decreased the stress hormone cortisol by 16% and increased the immune marker IgA, by 46%. This made me wonder. If it took four days to meditate in order to strengthen our immune systems by

46%, what might happen if we chanted Daimoku? What might happen even after just an hour of Daimoku?

I thought to myself that the power and energy of Fudō would surely manifest itself in an actual, concrete form. The capacity to heal our own bodies depends primarily on the proper functioning of our immune system. So I decided to measure immunoglobulin A (IgA), a protein marker indicating the strength of the immune system, both before and after chanting Daimoku for an hour.

IgA is an extraordinarily powerful protein, responsible for healthy immune function within our internal defense system. When it is activated, it is the protein at the frontline in the defense against infection and it is the primary indicator of our overall immunity capacity. It constantly fights bacteria, viruses, fungi or other organisms which penetrate our body or that have already entered our body. Research demonstrates that in this case increasing our IgA level is remarkably effective and much better than any flu shot or immune booster you might take.

Yet if our stress level increases and we experience negative emotions, such as fear, panic, anger or resentment, then this will lead to a fall in the IgA value and a weakened immune

Immunoglobulins attacking a virus

system. Research has shown that when stress levels rise, the levels of stress hormones like cortisol go up, this lowers levels of IgA. I realized that aside from their fear of catching the virus, everybody was feeling stress and panic at the prospect of losing their jobs or of having money problems in the immediate future. The virus led people to be paralyzed with fear. This would surely only lead to weakened immune systems in the population generally which would only aggravate the current crisis. So it was fortunate that we had asked ourselves only a couple of months previously: 'Could chanting Daimoku help to enhance the strength of our immune systems?'

I knew a medical practice which worked with a laboratory that could conduct such tests. We measured the concentration of this immune marker (IgA) before and after one hour of chanting Daimoku. We decided to measure from samples of saliva. The result truly surprised us.

The IgA value had increased by 54% only after one hour of Daimoku. Before I began to chant Daimoku, my IgA level had been at 128 mg/l. Yet this had increased to 198 mg/l after having chanted Daimoku for one hour.

Untersuchung	Ergebnis	Einheit		Vorwert	Referenzbereich/ Nachweisgrenze
Immunologie					
Sekretorisches IgA i. Speichel* Probenentnahme: 16:45 Uhr	128,0	mg/l			20,0 - 200,0
Sekretorisches IgA i. Speichel* Probenentnahme: 18:00 Uhr	198,0	mg/l		128,0	20,0 - 200,0

I was stunned and so was the laboratory where we had the measurements done. They were keen to know what I had been doing during that hour. What had increased my IgA level in such a dramatic way? The measurements demonstrated that you can radically boost your immune system by chanting Daimoku – a fact which helps us enormously during this time of pandemic.

Such a dramatic improvement of our immune function
Demonstrates how important the Buddhist practice of chanting
Daimoku is to increase and maintain
the fundamental conditions essential to good health.

So we can transform our physical state to a dramatic degree within one hour, by chanting Daimoku. This is also what my relative Sandy in the United States had experienced. Sandy had experienced the truly transformative power of chanting Daimoku.

Case Study 7:   Improving one's quality of life

Sandy had experienced a truly remarkable phenomenon, when her physical condition was transformed after she began chanting Daimoku and after having received a Gohonzon two years ago. Although she had suffered from numerous health problems, there was one particular thing that really bothered her: her body had simply stopped storing magnesium and consequently she required a magnesium IV-infusion every 3 to 4 days. The doctors did not know why this was so, but dependence on those magnesium infusions sometimes made life very difficult for Sandy. She could no longer travel the way she had previously and she needed to have a permanent access port in her chest where her magnesium dose could be administered. This was often painful and restricted her quality of life to a great degree. It was especially difficult to go on a vacation and to move around freely. This bothered her greatly.

When we went to visit her in April last year, we arranged an introduction for her to a regional SGI group. This way, she and her husband could more easily learn how to chant Daimoku. They quickly took it up and started going to group meetings regularly and finally received their Gohonzon a couple of months later. All this time, Sandy had been chanting regularly and was enjoying it more and more. At that point, she had one of the most interesting experiences.

All of a sudden, her body started to store magnesium once again, to such an extent that she no longer required the infusions. For the past four years, her life had been severely impacted by the need for these infusions. The doctors did not know why this had happened. They had no explanation for her body's ability to retain magnesium once again.

The permanent access port was removed from her chest and she was free to go on a holiday again without having to arrange for injections at her holiday resort. The only thing she had done differently, was chanting Daimoku, so Sandy was adamant that her new circumstances had come about through the practice of chanting. Now that she had overcome her most restricting condition, she knew that she could tackle her other health problems as well.

In my own practice, I realized that the transformative power of Fudo which can transform any physical suffering, can also manifest itself in a way that leads to the right medical consultant or person or substance which can heal or help to overcome illness and pain. I experienced this in China when by coincidence I was led to the right acupuncturist, who was able to heal the back pain I had suffered for the past two years, in just four weeks.

Transforming emotional pain

The figure of Aizen represents the principle of "transforming desire into enlightenment" (*Bonnō-soku-bodai*). Aizen, who in Sanskrit is called *Rāgarāja*, and who has three eyes and six arms, presents a most fearsome character. He holds a bow and arrow in his

hands. The red color of his body represents passionate attachment, which was traditionally considered to be the source of all
suffering. He therefore symbolizes this aspect of burning passion.
That´s why the color of his body is red. Yet he purifies all earthly
desires and frees all people from the illusions and suffering
caused by their earthly desires. The sun at his back, further symbolizes the determined resolve of his enlightened heart.

The principle of "transforming desire into enlightenment" refers
to the transformation of all emotional and psychological pain and
suffering. Most pain results from over-attachment to the people
we love and to things we possess. This was the main reason why I
had sought a Buddhist practice: I felt deeply the pain of having
lost my parents at a very early age. Having lost the actual home of
my parents, was also very painful, but made me realize that the
material possessions we acquire only give us an illusion of security. That´s when I suddenly realized that every relationship we
have here on earth is restricted to a certain time and place which
will inevitably end in its physical form - as we all die. Everyone
experiences this kind of pain at some point in life. After chanting
Daimoku, however, I no longer feel this pain. I can remember my
deceased relatives and friends without feeling sad. The sadness
does come back, however, but each time I transform it by chanting Daimoku, it loosens its grip on me and it returns with less
power. Further, the transformation principle of Aizen, can also
transform the negative emotions which otherwise might make us
ill or cause us suffering.

To chant Daimoku means to transform our emotions. Have you
ever felt the intense feeling of joy and the life-affirming, positive
attitude which you manifest after chanting? The more frequently
we evoke such feelings, the more we experience an emotional re-
encoding. The biophoton field around our body becomes more vibrant and much stronger. According to Dr. König, this is the moment when our positive emotions are being encoded and stored

in our biophoton field thus cancelling out our previously stored negative experiences. We start to become more emotionally independent, because we radiate happiness from deep within and thereby become less dependent on other people or on our outer circumstances.

We now understand that vitality, quality of life and awareness depend ultimately on the quantity and quality of the photons in our body.

If we are happy, it seems as if someone within us has turned on the light - our body then has a high concentration of biophotons, according to Dr. König. If the photons are highly ordered, i.e. coherent, they remain concentrated over a much longer period of time, like a laser beam. Then this state of happiness remains with us for much longer. But if the degree of order of the photon field is low, many photons are incoherent.

As a result, happiness is only a small flickering flame and never long lasting. In this case, the photons fan out and disperse like the beam of light from an ordinary flashlight. If we want to remain in our state of happiness, we need a lot of coherent photons – which create order and lasting harmony.

If we are unhappy or angry, on the other hand, this weakens our photon field, according to Dr. König. Biophoton emission is reduced and our energy field becomes more incoherent. It literally becomes much darker within ourselves. Dark feelings mean an absence of light.

Let´s take the emotion of anger, for example, which generally leads to a whole series of aggressive and destructive emotions like outrage, hate and the urge to take revenge. Such feelings of anger may seriously harm your physical health if they are not transformed: they are stored as unresolved emotions in your body.

Case Study 8:   Transforming sadness into joy

I especially remember the sudden change and emotional transformation of Sabita, a Nepalese woman whom I met when I
lived in Japan. I wanted to learn Japanese and enrolled on a
language course that was provided by the city of Kashiwa as a
support for foreigners. Sabita and I spent a lot of time together
before and after the Japanese language classes, when sometimes we would go shopping or have a cup of coffee together.

One morning I saw her waiting for me at the underground
station, but the look on her face was very sad and depressed. I
could actually feel the heavy pain in her heart, weighing down
her whole body. I asked her: "What is wrong with you, you
seem to be really unhappy today?" She almost began to cry and
told me that she was missing her little son whom she had had
to leave behind with her parents in Nepal; her husband had
found a research position at a university branch at Kashiwa city
where we lived, but he did not earn enough to be able to bring
their little boy with them to Japan. For them, life in Japan was
very expensive.

One day we went with another friend, an Iranian from the
language class, to buy a schoolbag for her little daughter as she
was about to begin her first year at school. In Japan schoolbags
are made out of real leather and they are very expensive. My
Iranian friend wanted to buy a good schoolbag for her daughter, so that she would not feel left out at school. That's when
my Nepalese friend almost began to cry again, as she realized
that she could never afford such an expensive schoolbag, even
if she found a way to bring her son to live with them in Japan.

I felt really sorry for her and encouraged her to chant Daimoku for a solution to her problem. She immediately agreed to
try to do so and came to my home where we chanted Daimoku
together for the first time. She really liked it and I invited her to
the local SGI Japanese group meeting, the zadankai. She was
warmly welcomed there by my Japanese friend Harumi, with
whom I chanted Daimoku each week.

So Sabita began to chant for a solution to be able to live together with her little son once again. She began to feel much better and far more optimistic after she began chanting and she and her husband even filled out the formal application in order to receive a gohonzon from the local Japanese group I had taken her to. And then something unexpected happened. Unexpectedly, two months after Sabita had begun to chant Daimoku regularly, her husband was offered a really well-paid research position at a Swedish university. This was the solution to their problem. A couple of months later, Sabita and her husband moved to Sweden. They could now afford to live together with their little son as a family once again.

I still remember Sabita's joyful face, with her radiant eyes, when she told me the news. Her prayer had been answered and she now appeared to be a completely different person, full of energy and laughter. Daimoku had been able to transform her deep emotional pain into joy and a vibrant hope for a better future.

The principle of transforming poison into medicine

The general designation for this kind of transformation is "transforming poison into medicine" (*Hendokuiyaku*) and essentially refers to the improvement in any life situation. Through the function of an elevated emotion which rises up when we chant Daimoku, and through the power of the energy of Daimoku, destructive emotions like for example anger can thereby be transformed, for example, into a heightened sensitivity to unfairness and injustice within society. This is a type of transformation where our ego-centered anger focused on personal issues can be redirected into an altruistic and compassionate effort to end the suffering of others. That's because we are more deeply aware of the suffering of other people when we chant Daimoku and we develop more compassion for their unhappy circumstances. After having chanted for some time, you may feel more intensely that we are all actually one; that we are all one consciousness.

Exercise

What is your experience with this type of transformation?

_____

When did you manage to transform any emotional attachment, for example?

_____

When did you manage to transform any dark feelings like sadness, anger or frustration into the feelings of joy and happiness by chanting Daimoku?

_____

When did you manage to transform any physical pain?

_____

The power of protection

The four heavenly kings

As well as the power of transformation there is another miracle principle which comes to life when we chant Daimoku to the Gohonzon. When the Mystic Law is activated, the "four heavenly kings" at each corner of the Gohonzon are also activated and manifest their protective function. If you take a close look at their iconographic depiction, you will see that they are trampling down evil demonic creatures with their feet (*see picture below*).

In this way they protect us from any malignant and evil attacks from outside.

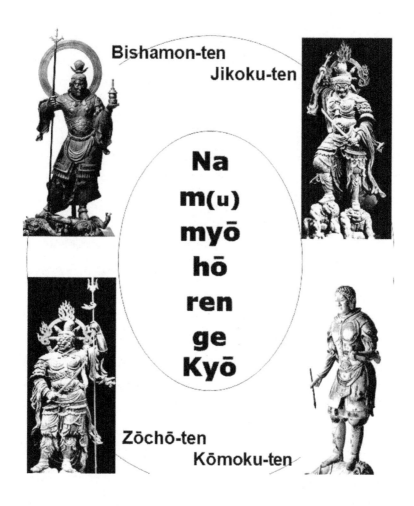

Bishamon-ten
Jikoku-ten

Na
m(u)
myō
hō
ren
ge
Kyō

Zōchō-ten
Kōmoku-ten

The protective mother Kishimojin and her Attendants

In addition to the heavenly kings, the Mandala Gohonzon includes representations of celestial bodies such as the Sun, the Moon and Venus, as well as pre-Buddhist Indian deities, such as Brahman, Indra, and Asura, who was originally a jealous and zealous enemy of all beings of heavenly light. Other demonic beings of Indian origin, such as *Kishimojin* (skr. Hāritī) and the ten Rakshasas

(*Jūrasetsunyo*) are also found inscribed on the Gohonzon. Nichiren often refers to these female demons in his writings, as they appear in Chapter 26, the "Dharani chapter", where they vow to protect all those who keep and recite the Lotus Sutra.

The relief of Hariti with her children on a wall of the ninth-century Buddhist temple Mendut, Java

Kishimojin, known as Hariti in pre-Buddhist times, was a cannibalistic nature spirit of a low rank, has now become transformed into a goddess who protects mothers and children. One day after having visited Ikegami temple, we passed a small temple where people were praying and making offerings. I asked my husband what kind of temple this might be, and he told me that it was a temple dedicated to *Kishimojin* and that people were praying to her for protection for their children. That's when I realized that for many Japanese *Kishimojin* represents a real protective power which they believe in.

Kishimojin with an infant. Kamakura period of 12th-13th century, Daigo-ji, Kyoto.

Against this historical background, it occurred to me that all the protective functions inscribed on the Gohonzon have taken on different forms and names depending on their cultural origins. The

loving and protective energy of *Kishimojin* should therefore be understood as a character personifying all the loving and protective energy of beings of light. For example, in the West, such beings are usually characterized as "angels".

The function of all these different forces is one and the same: to protect us or to help us fulfil our desires and to free us from all physical and emotional pain.

A protective Guardian Angel

We are not alone as we are surrounded and supported by all the protective and benevolent forces of the universe.

Thus, these deities and demons likewise function in their symbolic capacity as benevolent deities, as manifestations of the protective function of the universe itself (*Shotenzenjin*) in order to support us accomplishing our visions.

Unexpected support

So far, they are all symbolically represented, but their supportive and protective functions can also be carried out by certain other persons in some particular circumstances. Such experiences are related intrinsically through "mystical coincidence of synchronicity" which we can normally neither plan nor control by your ordinary conscious mind.

This means, when we chant Daimoku, we are protected, supported and guided by cosmic consciousness in ways we could never conceive of ourselves. And a protective function can be manifested through a friend or even a stranger who appears just at the right time to help you. Chanting Daimoku brings us into coherence with cosmic consciousness which then brings the right people into our lives in line with this coherence

Case Study 9:   Protection from disaster

I experienced this two years ago when we had a problem with the ceiling of our living room. There had been some water leaking from the ceiling which suggested there was a leak from the balcony of the loft. By now there was already a hole in the ceiling and we were afraid that the leakage would lead to mould growth along the ceiling. We let this hole dry out and decided to have it repaired later. That morning whilst chanting, I was thinking about which company we should call in order to fix the problem but I could not think of anyone appropriate. I decided to ask a friend whether she had an idea which company would be best given the situation.

Later that day, I decided to go to town and have my hair cut. I went to my Vietnamese hairdresser and she told me that at that moment, she did not have time but suggested I came back an hour later. There was another Vietnamese friend of hers sitting there and he asked me when I left: But you are coming back later, aren´t you? I confirmed that I would be back later. When I returned, I still had to wait for a couple of minutes and the same guy was still sitting there and he started a conversation with me. It turned out it he was a craftsman with his own company and that as it was his day off, he was visiting all his other Vietnamese friends. I told him about our problem with the hole in the ceiling and the leaking water and he confirmed he would be able to fix it. Thus we arranged for him to come around the next day to have a look at the ceiling and the leaking balcony.

He started to work on the problem and soon discovered that the whole balcony was already soaking with water internally. He opened it all up and fixed it. He found out that if he had not discovered the problem at that point, the wood would have broken and we would have had a real problem with mould spreading everywhere. This would have rendered our house worthless and irreparable. The problem was solved just in time to avoid any permanent damage. The curious thing was that the full extent of the problem was not visible from the outside.

This Vietnamese craftsman turned out to be a real blessing as he offered so many solutions to a variety of problems we were experiencing with the house. He also helped us to rebuild the apartment downstairs so we could rent it out. Hiring an ordinary company would have meant waiting for some weeks and paying thousands of euros to have all this work done, yet he offered us his help at a reasonable price.

After that, he became a good friend of ours. When we needed his help, he would come to us in one or two days even though he had much other work to do. Additionally, he always charged a reasonable price. Once again, I experienced the deep intuition? that I had been guided and directed to this craftsman who saved our house and our contented existence.

Exercise

You must have experienced such protective and supportive functions of the universe based on your Buddhist practice. In what form did they appear? What did they look like? Can you describe how a situation unfolded and what the result of it was?

- -

What was the starting situation?

- -

Who or what played a role in the process?

_ _

What was the result?

_ _

Chanting Daimoku before the Mandala Gohonzon activates
all the supportive and protective functions of the universe
to enable special circumstances which allow the mystic
coincidence of synchronicity to occur in your favor.

Chapter 7
Myō-Hō,
the law of potentiality and actuality

> There is an infinite potentiality that characterizes the whole cosmos. There is a cosmic consciousness our individual consciousness participates in. — *Lothar Schäfer*

We are always in communication with the universe

I slowly began to understand that my external circumstances had something to do with my inner state of consciousness. When I started chanting Daimoku I regarded it at first as an experiment and wanted to see whether making internal changes through this practice would have a noticeable effect on my life. In the meantime I realized that when I get stuck in life, I really need to look at the thoughts which occupy me all the time, especially how I habitually act each day, as well as what emotions I habitually feel.

The compassionate life force of the universe yearns to know what we desire to create each moment of every day. So if you remember that your energy is being broadcast out at every moment, then it follows that there is an intelligent life force energy which is receiving our broadcast and responding to it. It continually receives and responds to our energy.

We are all energy towers broadcasting signals which the universe responds to at every moment of every day. The energy which creates all things is dynamically flowing through us. Yet we are born with the power to direct it. The question is: how should we direct it?

Living in a quantum universe

Do you recall the quantum field which was described in our first book »Transform your energy- change your life- Nichiren Buddhism 3.0«? According to the spiritual quantum model of Dr. Joe Dispenza, this is a level of pure potential beyond space and time. There everything already exists as energetic potential. All potential experiences exist there as energetic frequency patterns in the infinite "sea of all potentials".

But the most astonishing thing is that this energetic quantum field seems to react to consciousness. It exists in a constant state of unlimited possibility, while each possibility is seeking to "become form" or to "materialize" or manifest through the influence of consciousness. We don't live in a Newtonian clockwork-like mechanical universe, we live in a quantum universe fundamentally grounded in consciousness.

And according to scientific researcher Dawson Church, a quantum universe is a set of possibilities which are susceptible to influence by many factors, including thought, will and intention. That's the case as scientists have now confirmed that consciousness is energy as well.

All of our thoughts, ideas, emotions and intentions are
actually energy.

Our reality is multi-dimensional

A world of potentiality is obviously a completely different world with its own laws and ways of being, and the fascinating thing is that this "other world" is directly interwoven with our own actuality, like two sides of a single page. Consequently, what we perceive with our senses represents not simply the expression of some hidden power or energy, but at a more profound level, the actual manifestation of cosmic consciousness itself, which ultimately underlies all phenomena.

Further, it is our own individual consciousness, through the manifestation of our own thoughts and feelings, which provides the template through which our own local understanding of reality is mediated to this cosmic consciousness. We tend to view our actions as the primary means for accomplishing our goals. We always think that first we must take action and then we'll gain benefit from that action. But when we have more understanding of the subtler realm of consciousness, we become aware that the opposite is in fact more effective. For we can align ourselves in thought, emotion and energy with our desired outcomes while we chant, and this draws us to those actions which support their unfolding. That's when we take action; because we are genuinely inspired rather than acting out of enforced obligation or blind activism.

After many years of chanting Daimoku, I realized that if we want to change our outer circumstances, we must change *from the inside out*. But what exactly does the simultaneous existence of two separate states mean?

Myō-Hō or we live in a world of dual-aspect

I remember that the main reason why I started looking for a spiritual practice was the pain caused by the deaths of many family members. Things were constantly changing. Somehow I found it difficult to handle this. I had to come to terms with the fact that dying is a life process we all have to go through.

One important aspect of the Mystic Law (*Myō-Hō*) is surely the "principle of cause and effect" according to which all phenomena are subject to change and don't remain the same as time passes. This insight into the ephemeral nature of our lives and the world around us, grounds the fundamental teachings of Buddha Shakyamuni.

Thus, the causality principle is inherently related to the aspects of life and death, or in more general terms to the aspects of actuality and potentiality and of existence and non-existence. The reality surrounding us, which includes the material form of all things, is subject to the constant change between potentiality and actuality.

This is always clear to me whenever I look outside and watch the big tree in front of my living room window. In summer it is really green and full of leaves that fall in autumn. In winter there are no leaves on the tree, but I know definitely that they will return the following summer in exactly the same way that they did the year before. The potential in the form of information, is there. In winter, the leaves have returned to a state of potentiality; in summer they can be viewed fully manifest. Nichiren observed this cycle of nature too:

> Plants and trees are withered and bare in autumn and winter, but when the sun of spring and summer shines on them, they put forth branches and leaves, and then flowers and fruit.
> *The Daimoku of the Lotus Sutra,* WND I: 146

The same principle applies to all people. It is always a shock to me when someone dies. Suddenly, a person with whom we talked yesterday; who we could see, hear, feel and touch, is no longer there. Yet we still feel a deep connection to that person. He or she has returned to his or her potential state. That's why "*myō*" also means "death" and "*hō*" also means "life".

> *Myō* represents death, and *hō*, life. Living beings that pass through the two phases of life and death are the entities of the Ten Worlds, or the entities of Myoho-renge-kyo.
> [...] Here "living beings and their environments" means the phenomena of life and death. Thus, it is clear that, where life and death exist, cause and effect, or the Law of the lotus, is at work.
> The Great Teacher Dengyō states, "The two phases of life and death are the wonderful workings of one mind. The two ways

> of existence and nonexistence are the true functions of an in-
> herently enlightened mind."
>   No phenomena—either heaven or earth, yin or yang, the sun
> or the moon, the five planets, or any of the worlds from hell to
> Buddhahood—are free from the two phases of life and death.
> Life and death are simply the two functions of Myoho-renge-
> kyo.   *The heritage of the ultimate law of life*, WND I, p.216

Thus, Myō-Hō represents the law of constant change which applies to all phenomena: from the emptiness of the state of potentiality to the actuality of the state of manifestation, and vice versa.
Being aware of this simple fact of our daily life, will make us more
sensitive about our relationship to the so-called "real world" in
which we live. It is not as solid as it appears; it is not fixed or un-
changeable. This dual-aspect of our reality becomes even more
vivid when we understand potentiality in terms of energy.

The energy dimension behind material reality

Are you aware that every time we perceive physical, material reality, we also interact with an invisible reality? Did you know that
we ourselves have an invisible dimension? This invisible dimension is just as "real" as the physical dimension which we perceive
with our senses. Let's look at a hand for example. Most of us
would probably identify with the picture of the hand on the left,
just because we are accustomed to it. The picture on the right,
however, is just as "real". It's a photograph of the energetic field.
Everyone has an energetic field, yet most people are unaware of
it.

What is usually most difficult to understand is that we have both
a physical dimension and an energetic dimension which exist *at
the same time*. Of course, reality has several dimensions. There is
both a physical you and an energetic you. What we see on the
outside is the physical world. But energy is the underlying force
which drives all things. It's the activating force which is behind

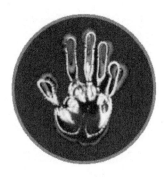

Visible aspect (Hō)   Invisible aspect (Myō)

everything that is physical. We experience that energy in two distinct ways. On the one hand, we can experience and seek to
change the physical world which we see, smell, hear, touch, taste
and feel. That's what we all try to do each day. We think we know
exactly how to do that. On the other hand, the energy dimension
to the world is not that obvious to our senses.

Our energy field reveals our physical condition

Dr. Valerie Hunt, professor at UCLA (University of California, Los
Angeles) was one of the first scientists to demonstrate the existence of the human energy field by way of high frequency record-
ings taken in her laboratory at UCLA. She proved that this field
changes dynamically depending on the physical condition and the

emotions and motiva-
tions of a person who is
interacting with the en-
ergy radiation from ob-
jects and other living
beings. The emotions
we experience mani-
fest in our energy field.

   This picture shows a
warm-hearted,   loving

relationship between a mother and her child. You can see that the energy fields of the mother and child overlap in a harmonious way.

Dr. Hunt was also one of the first scientists who paid attention to the relationship between changes in our biofield and our health. She considered that physical symptoms manifest due to a disturbance in our energy field. Consequently, if we can correct the disturbance in our energy field, physical symptoms of any disorder should disappear.

According to Hunt, if we wish to heal our body, we must intervene at the level of the energy field; at the level of the blueprint, so to speak. If we intervene only physically, by the means of surgery or medication, for instance, without modifying the blueprint, then whatever condition we are suffering from will simply remanifest.

Along with other scientists, she claimed that the energy field around your body actually serves as a template which determines what manifests in our physical body and in our lives. There would even appear to be evidence that interferences in a person's energy field might well precede any injury or accident which a person suffers later.

Hunt suggests that this energy field contains an imprint of our early life experiences, of our inherited illnesses, even of our memories before we were born. The energy field organizes our current actuality. It choreographs our life experience unless we can purify the imprints in our energy field.

For Dr. Valerie Hunt, all of our limitations are a consequence of an incoherent bioenergy field, and when we balance our energy field, we thereby become fully functional human beings. Health, energy, creativity, our psychological and physical condition— all are aspects of our human potential. We limit our potential by the way we choose to handle our emotions, sometimes creating incoherent energy patterns which block or distort the flow of energy through our energy field.

Dr. Hunt claims that our perception is colored by the flow and dynamism of the energy in our energy field and especially the emotional energy which is its organizing principle. This means if we want to change our physical state, we have to change our energy field first. That's exactly what we do when we chant Daimoku for we are aware that chanting Daimoku brings coherence to our energy field.

It is the energy field which creates and influences physical reality and not the other way around.

Exercise

Ask yourself – Are you the kind of person who tends to worry a lot? Or are you usually pretty calm? This should tell you how coherent or incoherent your energy field is.

Energy change occurs first

When we measured our energy fields while chanting, we used the GDV device that was invented by the Russian professor, Korotkov. This device measures the biophoton emission of our body which actually consists of tiny bits of light. Our measure-

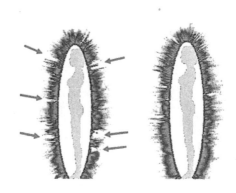

Increased energy field after ten minutes of chanting daimoku

ments demonstrated that our biophoton emission increases while chanting.

Now imagine chanting Daimoku in front of the Gohonzon. Don't we normally become more aware of the energy both in our body and in our surrounding environment? Don't we feel that we are filled with the energy of Daimoku and that our whole body is vibrating at a harmonious and pleasant frequency? Once we feel the energy changes in our body and our environment after chanting Daimoku, we learn that transforming our energy is actually much easier than trying to change the things external to us in the physical world.

As discussed earlier, our bodies are surrounded by invisible fields of electromagnetic energy. But if we keep living in a state of ongoing stress, we keep drawing upon an invisible field of energy, says Dr. Joe Dispenza. For we are constantly drawing energy from this field and turning it into chemistry. The more we do this, the more the electromagnetic field around our body will deplete.

As a result, we diminish our light and we have no energy left to put our visions into practice and to create a new life. This point is fundamental as far as the nature of our visions and intentions is concerned. In order to create a new life, we need the electromagnetic energy around our body. That´s because our visions and intentions require electromagnetic energy, as research has demonstrated. It seems that in order to have a strong and clear vision for our life

 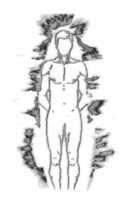

Normal Light Field   Diminished Light Field

we need to draw upon the electromagnetic field of our body.

The principle of *Myō-Hō* demonstrates that energy manifests in the physical, material world. If we want to change the visible, physical world, we must change the energy dimension first. But most people are only focused on changing the things which are external to themselves. They ignore their energy dimension.

We must align to what we want energetically first.

Dual reality

**The unvisible reality full of
possibilities beyond time and space**

**The material reality with
space-time-dimension**

Chapter 8
Observing reality

> Because our consciousness notices everything, it observes and pays attention to us. It is aware of our thoughts, our dreams, our behavior, and our desires. It "observes" everything into physical form.
>
> —*Joe Dispenza*

The principle of particle-duality in quantum physics

We do not live in a solid, inert world of matter but in a vital world full of energy and dynamic change. As explored in the previous chapter, the term *Myōhō* therefore indicates the dual nature of life and the world as understood in terms of life and death, energy and matter, or in a more general sense, of potentiality and actuality. And the most fascinating thing is that this dual aspect is also characteristic of the subatomic level of matter.

All quanta like photons and electrons have this dual aspect of being both a wave and a particle. What really interests us in this respect, is not just an understanding of the nature of quanta, but rather the question of how our consciousness affects the external world around us. When we seek evidence of how this occurs, it is astonishing to discover how much scientific evidence there is, in fact. Among other things, there are a series of particular experiments known as the "double-slit experiment" which led to a new discovery termed the "observer effect": this provides substantial evidential support to the general claim that "mind can change matter."

Initially, the double-slit experiment was conducted at the beginning of the 19th Century in order to determine the nature of light. It had already been demonstrated that light had the character of a wave. Later, through further experiments, it was demonstrated that light also had the character of a particle. Given this, it became commonly understood that light has the dual aspect of being either a wave or a particle. In the course of the dramatic development of quantum mechanics since the 1920s, scientists have discovered the strange phenomenon that "quanta collapse waves into particles when they are being observed." This discovery has led some to conclude that our conscious intentions can directly impact on physical reality. Well, let's take a closer look at this phenomenon known as the "observer effect."

The observer effect in the double-slit experiment

To begin, let's imagine throwing some tennis balls at a wall with two slits in it. Some of the tennis balls will bounce off the wall, but some will go through the slits. Once they have passed through the slits, the balls will hit a screen that is registering their trajectories. What should we expect to observe? Wouldn't we expect to see two patterns of trajectories each of roughly the same pattern as the two slits? That's right. That's exactly what we do see.

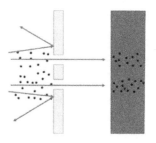

But now let's consider this example at the subatomic level and instead of tennis balls, let's fire quanta such as photons and electrons at a plate with two slits with a screen behind it to record their trajectories. Bear in mind that we know already that a photon has the dual aspect of being understood as both a wave and a particle simultaneously. Shouldn't we expect the photons to behave exactly like the tennis balls? Shouldn't we expect to observe two patterns of trajectories roughly the same shape as the two slits?

Well, the surprising thing is that this time, this is not the case. For we now see several stripes on the back screen. This pattern re-sembles the wave-like 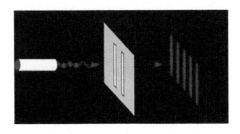 ripple effect produced when a ball is thrown into water through a wall with two slits.

This is because the moving photons pass through the slits in the form of two waves, each spreading out from each of the slits. The two waves then ei-ther reinforce each other or cancel each other out thereby showing a definite "in- 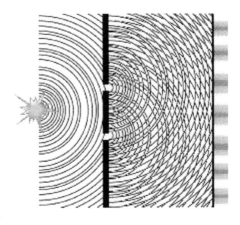 terference pattern." This typical feature of a wave interaction is evidenced by the varied patterns registered on the back screen.

At this point a question arises: Is each photon passing through only one slit or through both slits at the same time? This question can't be answered because the instant a scientist installs a meas-uring instrument to observe what's happening, the scientist no longer observes a wave pattern. Instead, something stranger was discovered. The instant a measuring instrument is installed, the photons and electrons which have been fired at the plate only register as particles and are recorded in two distinctive stripes with roughly the same shape as the two slits. A wave pattern is no longer observed, for the photons and electrons now only register as particles.

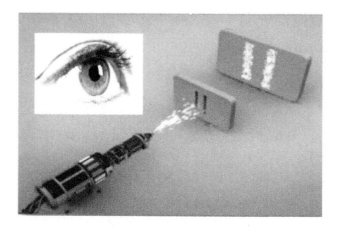

Quanta behave like particles when they are being observed.
This phenomenon is called the "observer effect"
which collapses the wave function into particles.

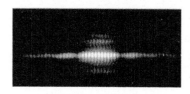 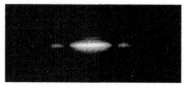

Quanta produce a wave pattern of interference when they are not being observed.	Quanta show up as single particles when they are being observed.

This experiment essentially demonstrates that if quanta, such as photons and electrons, are fired at a plate with two slits, they behave as waves when they are not being observed. Yet as soon as they are observed, they behave as particles.

This discovery was groundbreaking, because in classical physics, it was not believed that the process of measurement or observation of itself could influence the outcome in any way.

Are we observing our own reality?

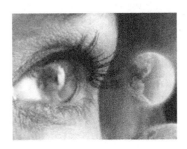 The scientific explanation behind all this is that subatomic particles exist in a state of *potentiality* until they are observed. Before they are observed, subatomic particles merely have the potential to become something definite and material. Applying this insight from the double-slit experiment, we may come to the conclusion that it is *our* expectations, our own focus and observation, which enables subatomic particles to manifest as concrete objects. Consequently, these experimental findings indicate a whole new dimension to the role of consciousness!

The "observer effect" demonstrates the primary role of the human observer in influencing the behavior of quanta, and from this, we can conclude we are constantly influencing and transforming reality at the quantum or subatomic level.

The double-slit experiments suggest that consciousness is influencing the material world around us all the time.

In her book "the intention experiment" (which considers the question of how human intention affects matter), Lynne McTaggart summarizes the practical implications of the observer effect as follows:

Living consciousness is somehow central to this process of transforming the unconstructed quantum world into something resembling everyday reality.   - *Lynne McTaggart*

The observer effect shows us in a dramatic way how closely mind and matter are inter-connected. Particles appear according to the expectations of the observer. When the observer is no longer present, they return to their wave function and become a cloud of possibilities once more.

Exercise

Is there one particular part of your life or situation in your life where you would like to have a whole cloud of possibilities available to you once again?

_ _

Write down one or two presumptions or expectations with which you might habitually and automatically consider such a situation:

_ _

If there is an infinite number of potentials and opportunities within the field of cosmic consciousness to which we have access while chanting, are there one or more ways by which this situation could be solved optimally?

_ _

Do mind and matter interact?

As shown above, the "observer effect" highlights the importance of the human observer in influencing the behavior of quanta and implies that we are constantly transforming reality at the quantum or subatomic level.

However, many materialist scientists radically disagree with such an interpretation, arguing that the experiment is not at all about a human being making a particular personal observation, but rather that the observation is being made by a machine; an automated, inactive material detector - which only analogously "observes" the event. The mind-matter interaction is, therefore, simply considered to be mere speculation. Indeed, such scientists are skeptical that human conscious intention in itself could result in an "observer effect". It is considered far more likely that such an effect is simply a result of a physical intervention by an automated measuring instrument which thereby "collapses waves into particles".

This whole debate has led Dr. Dean Radin, chief scientist at the Institute of Noetic Sciences (IONS), to ask some fundamental questions: Should the "observer" be only a machine designed to detect the presence of photons, or should the observer actually be a human observer, who is alone capable of collapsing the wave-function? Can focused human intention in itself have a physical impact on material reality?

While raising such questions, he is clearly aware of the bias towards "common sense" in physics, which normally seeks to exclude the factor of consciousness in any consideration of material reality. He is critical of this particular scientific prejudice, which is found throughout the established natural sciences, and which downplays the role of human conscious intention as follows:

> The notion that consciousness may be related to the formation of physical reality has come to be associated more with medieval magic and so-called New Age ideas than it is with sober science. [...] For more than 50 years such studies were considered unsuitable for serious investigators.
>
> *Consciousness and the double-slit interference pattern:*
> *Six experiments*, Phys. Essays 25, 2 (2012), p. 170

Further, Dr. Radin did not only begin to investigate the role of human conscious intention and the "observer effect"; he also tried to find an answer to the question as to whether a particular state of consciousness was required in order to produce such an effect. In short, he expressly asked whether experienced meditators could affect the outcome of the double slit experiment in a more immediate and significant way than those observers with no meditation experience.

That explains why in 2012, Dr. Radin conducted experiments to expressly determine whether conscious attention can indeed affect the interference pattern of a classic double-slit setup. His team tested 137 people in 6 experiments, involving a total of 250 sessions and another 250 control sessions without observers. With extremely high statistical reliability, the results demonstrated that awareness can indeed do just that!

The results confirmed that meditators were able to cause a significant shift from an expected wave pattern, enabling the identification of many solitary particles when, normally, only particles acting as waves should have been observed. Consequently, the meditators had caused a highly significant collapse of the wavefunction. Radin also found that experienced meditators caused a more noticeable shift than non-meditators.

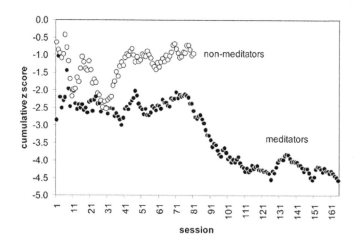

He then conducted a further 5,000 sessions with experienced meditators, and 7,000 sessions with a computer functioning as a control. The sessions held by the computer had no effect whatsoever, but the meditators caused a highly significant collapse of the wave-function. It was focused human intention which appeared to "collapse the wave into a particle".

In fact, this experiment can be conducted by a measuring instrument alone or by a human experimenter simply observing the particles. Research has demonstrated that an actual, live human being has a much better effect than any automated device in recording the behavior of photons and electrons. The "conscious intention" of a human being seems to be more powerful than the electromagnetic impulse of a measuring instrument in influencing the outcome.

Radin also hooked up the meditators to an EEG to monitor their brain activity while they were achieving the best results during the double slit experiment. The EEG tests provided further evidence that when participants were concentrating with the greatest intensity and focus, their ability to affect the outcome of the double-slit experiment increased. Conversely, when they were no longer so focused, their capacity to affect the outcome was reduced.

Radin´s research shows that it is not our everyday state of consciousness which is able to "collapse a wave into a particle". It takes a more deeply focused and altered state of Consciousness to achieve this.

We are the creators of our own reality

Applying the insight that mind and matter interact with each other, to our daily practice of chanting Daimoku, we conclude that a prayer is an intention which can collapse the vast number of possibilities into the reality of actuality. Potential states and experiences in the energy field, can manifest as actual states and experiences in the physical world. The more we intensify our intention in prayer, the more likely it is, that it will be realized. In this way, chanting can assist in transmuting a mere possibility into a more certain probability. This principle is expressed by the two characters of *Myō-Hō*. Chanting enables us to activate this mechanism.

Dual reality

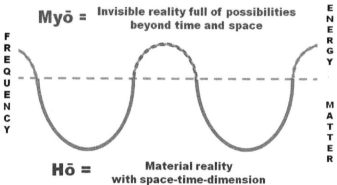

Myō = Invisible reality full of possibilities beyond time and space

Hō = Material reality with space-time-dimension

In this process, it does not matter how seemingly impossible the desired outcome appears to be. The observer effect implies that if we do not make any effort to create our world with our own particular personal vision and intentions, then we are restricted to the reality of our own surroundings. Without our own vision, our 'reality' is influenced and controlled by the intentions and vision of the society in which we live, of our family (through our family karma), our genes and (by the way our parents and ancestors have lived their lives and died).

If you don't express your wishes and take responsibility for your own life, others will decide your destiny!

The observer effect also demonstrates that reality is malleable. Chanting Daimoku in the state of coherent mind will release the fixation of our ordinary, local mind with ordinary, local reality and instead, radically realign our restricted mind into coherence and harmony with an unlimited, non-local mind. This is when we can expand our potential and manifest that power which can achieve the extraordinary.

For as Nichiren tells us, we need the power of our subconscious  mind and even more, the power of non-local consciousness or pure consciousness, in order to actually realize or attain our wishes. This is what Nichiren had in mind when he drew for us the analogy of a fly clinging to a horse's tail.

> A blue-bottle fly, if it clings to the tail of a thoroughbred horse, can travel ten thousand miles.
> *On Establishing the Correct Teaching*, WND I: 17

That's when we let go of the illusion that we are only isolated, local entities. We are at one with the universal mind and all the friction which we experience at the level of our local, restricted mind, falls away. Life becomes easier and things begin to flow. The kind of life we create from such a universal perspective, is radically different in kind to the life we create when we think that we are only isolated, local selves.

Daimoku is a most powerful bearer of our dreams, visions and intentions!

Exercise

How much of your attention is focused on things, situations or people fixed in the material reality every day?

_ _

How much of your attention is focused on the vast field of possibility while chanting?

_ _

How much attention do you pay to your energy field? Remember: if you change your energy, you can transform your life.

_ _

Chapter 9
Opening up to cosmic consciousness

Our environment is a mirror reflecting our own consciousness

Let´s come back to the observer effect. What does the discovery of the observer effect mean for our own actual lives? Researchers have concluded that we are by no means simply the passive observers which we normally assume ourselves to be, but rather that the content, nature and energy of our own consciousness is reflected in the multiple manifestations of things in the actual world around us.

How would our lives change if we could intentionally utilize the observer effect to "collapse" limitless potential into one particular desired actuality?

Have we really become familiar with the idea that mind and matter are inseparable? How often do we forget this fundamental aspect when we try to change the circumstances of, or the people in, our lives? Do we rather wait in the hope that external circumstances will change to our advantage, although we ourselves feel that we have almost no control over our own external circumstances?

The principle of *Eshōfuni* tells us that what we experience in the external, manifested world is a direct reflection of what we are experiencing within the internal world of our own consciousness. This is because as human beings we exist in multiple dimensions simultaneously. There is part of us which exists in physical form and which takes physical, concrete action. But underlying this physical aspect of ourselves, is a non-physical essence, which is

the inner realm where our thoughts, emotions, perceptions, beliefs and desires are formed. In fact, consciousness gives life to
that which is concrete. Our physical surroundings, therefore, are
a visible manifestation of our moment-to-moment internally experienced reality. The principle of *Eshōfuni* tells us that our inner
world and outer world is inseparable and that each interacts with
the other, so that our surroundings influence our inner experience
while our inner experience also influences our external circumstances.

Exercise

Do you think that your inner state influences your outer reality?

-- --

Are you still seeking something outside of yourself in order to
change how you feel inside?

-- --

How do we see other people?

The "observer-effect" implies that everything which we experience as reality has been shaped by our own observations. This
principle also applies to how we see and experience other people.
Have you ever considered that the way other people behave towards us has something to do with the way *we* see them? Let's
take our spouse or our children, for example. If we see them as
stupid, *we* are creating them that way. If we see them as brilliant,
we are also creating them that way.

I remember a conversation with a neurofeedback expert we
went to see to have our brain waves measured (while chanting
Daimoku). He told me that experiments had been carried out
which demonstrated clearly that the notion or expectation a

teacher has about a child, significantly influences the performance of that child. In one experiment, a teacher was told that for the next couple of hours, he would work with a child who had some learning difficulties, especially relating to math's. In fact, this was not true at all, as previously the child had been performing exceptionally well especially in math's. However, when working with this teacher, the child suddenly had difficulties understanding even the most basic tasks given to him. It was obvious that it had been the teacher's expectations that had led to a "learning block" in the child's brain. This implies that what we think about others actually affects their behavior and performance, to a significant degree.

Yet it doesn't appear that way when we look out at the world only from the perspective of our ordinarily limited five senses. Then, it seems that there is a definite, objective reality "out there". The people and things around us seem to be wholly separate from us. How often have we had thoughts such as: `my boss is really unreliable` or `this friend of mine is so selfish`? How often have we had thoughts such as: 'my husband/ wife will never change; forget it`! However, what we forget is that in an observer-based reality, we are highly likely to find just what we are looking for. In fact, the most important question is: 'what are *we* looking for'?

Exercise

Can you train yourself to deliberately look for the best in the people within your social world?

_ _

Are you focusing on something that you want or something that you don't want?

_ _

Are you focusing on the circumstances of a conflict with someone else or on building a more harmonious relationship with that person?

_____

Try to switch your focus to what you want and away from what you don't want.

_____

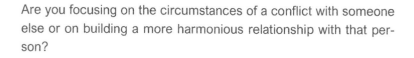

The echo of our past thoughts and beliefs

I have noticed that whenever people have a new vision for themselves, or develop a new intention while chanting, e.g. "I am going to find another job", or "I am going to lose weight" or "I am going to change my relationship with this person", then to begin with, they tend to be really passionate. We are determined and absolutely sure that we are going to change this particular aspect of our lives. We are on fire! We keep chanting for a particular goal. Things seem to be progressing towards the desired outcome. We complete job applications, we begin a new diet, we behave differently. But then we are challenged. This always seems to be the case. We are doing fine on our diet and then a friend invites us to a special meal that is more than tempting. The old echo of whatever we have been doing, thinking or feeling before, is now coming back and testing us. We re-experience our old habitual ways of thought and feeling. Old belief patterns might resurface. "You are just not lucky in your relationships" or "you will never be really happy", or "it is much more difficult for women to be successful than for men".

However, I have realized that whatever comes up, is exactly that which stops us progressing. Our old fears might show up again. That's when we need to be consistent and double our efforts to change our own personal frequency by chanting Daimoku. This is when it helps to tell ourselves while chanting: "yes, this is actually who I wish to become". Indeed, I have realized that in those particular moments we are being challenged to maintain our new vision and frequency in the face of the powerful reflection of our old habitual reality. It is certainly a test. If we cannot maintain our new frequency while listening to echoes from the past, of how we used to think and feel, then we will never be able to handle our new reality. And we now recognize, that whenever we resolve on a new intention or direction for ourselves, there will be an echo from the past. Our partner may question our decision to change our job and might tell us that it is too risky. Or our friends might try to pull us back and prevent us from moving on. Or our car breaks down. Such things may well reawaken our own doubts and we might think: "be more realistic". I have had such hopes and intentions before but things never turned out the way I wished". But if we give up at this point, then our hopes and intentions can never become reality.

After years of chanting, I have learnt that if we face an obstacle after having set a new vision or intention, it actually means that we are in fact progressing in a positive way - in the sense that a previous negative belief or habit is exposed (and ultimately, addressed) as that which has always been a hindrance to us. Whatever needs to be addressed and transformed will show up. This might be old negative thought patterns and feelings of unworthiness or a lack of self-belief. So we must hold on to our new vision or intention at all costs. We must uproot our negative beliefs and see them as opportunities for positive self-transformation. We must believe in the Gohonzon more than in any of our negative beliefs. Then our new vision will truly emerge in actuality.

Exercise

After setting a new intention while chanting, what old beliefs, thoughts and feelings surfaced as obstacles to hinder the actualization of your new vision?

Decide on a positive state of being which you intend to make manifest, such as:

☐ I am vibrantly healthy.

☐ I am living in abundance.

☐ I am happy.

☐ I am especially worthy.

☐ I am well-organized.

Notice the thoughts and emotions that are also surfacing with each of these intentions. Are there also negative thoughts such as: "I am too old/young/fat/thin/stupid to be or do this? Or "I am not worthy"?

Notice that these are just limiting beliefs and not unchanging truths. Do not let them define you but focus again on your original intention as that which most truly defines your reality.

Do such thoughts and emotions fit the future you wish to enjoy? Write down some of the thoughts that you do NOT want to think anymore in the future (e.g. I can't do it. I'm not good enough. I will make mistakes. This part of my life is terrible, will never change,...)

Cosmic consciousness is observing us

When we surrender to the universal Mystic Law represented on the Gohonzon, we surrender to a greater intelligence which is intimately aware of us and which is observing us. It simply knows our desires and wishes. It knows what we are thinking and feeling all day long. Whenever we experience it while chanting Daimoku to the Gohonzon, we begin to feel connected to everyone, everything and every place. Sometimes you just have to let go after setting an intention in order to let cosmic consciousness work things out for you. Just stop thinking about the "How" your dreams will become true. If you surrender the "How" to life's magic, it will occur more swiftly. You just have to trust. Cosmic consciousness knows your intention and can observe it becoming a reality. It can arrange things for you, which you would never be able to arrange yourself. The question is: Can you open up to cosmic consciousness?

Case study 10: Cosmic consciousness is observing you

I experienced this principle very intensely during one of my stays in Japan. At that time, I felt a deep desire to see a "real" Nichiren Gohonzon. I really wanted to see an "original" of Nichiren himself; a Gohonzon which he had inscribed himself. Nichiren himself had become so familiar and so real to me in the previous years, I wanted to feel his energy even closer and stronger and wondered all the time how I could see an original Gohonzon, autographed by Nichiren himself. I also wanted to see an original Gosho; one of the writings Nichiren himself had written. I knew that his script »*Risshō Ankoku Ron* (On Establishing the Correct Teaching for the Peace of the Land)« was issued at the temple of Nakayama Hokekyōji, which is one of the main temples of the Toki Jōnin lineage, on November 4th every year, but I had never been able to attend on that date. Yet I was determined to get back as far as possible to the original source from which everything had originated.

My husband Yukio did me a favor and called various institutions that might make it possible to see such a Gohonzon. We were told again and again that, unfortunately, an originally inscribed Nichiren Gohonzon was rarely open to a general public viewing, for only on very rare special occasions would such a Gohonzon be displayed publicly. Unfortunately, we were told, this was not one of those times. Consequently, I gave up my efforts and decided that I was not likely to see a Nichiren-Gohonzon at that point, yet there remained a kind of yearning within my consciousness to see one at some time. But I let go of this desire, believing it could not be fulfilled.

On the last day of our stay in Japan, Yukio and I decided to drive to Kamakura again because we found out there was a place there which had been the location of Shijō Kingo's house. On that day, we made very slow progress. We wanted to pass through Tokyo and then continue towards Kamakura. But the traffic was slow and heavy and it took longer than expected just to drive through Tokyo. Thus, we realized that we would not have enough time to drive to Kamakura and back, that day. We thought about which way to go and my husband suddenly took a road that turned slightly to the left. In the end, we had to stop in front of a traffic light that was on red. Right there, was a large sign to the left of the traffic light with the imprint: *Ikegami Honmonji*, the temple of the Ikegami brothers. We had not planned this at all, but having seen the sign, we decided spontaneously to visit the Temple of the Ikegami brothers, rather than going on to Kamakura. This had happened completely by chance.

When we arrived, there was a very great surprise awaiting me: a three-day exhibition of Nichiren's original Gohonzons and Gosho had opened on that very day. These extremely rare and precious items

were otherwise completely inaccessible to the public. I could hardly believe my luck: my wish had been fulfilled; we had been led straight to where I found exactly what I had focused on in my consciousness for weeks! I got the chance to see several original gohonzons and goshos personally inscribed and enrolled by Nichiren. I felt the invincible energy of this great master flow from his actual, distinctive handwriting. Nichiren had become absolutely real for me.

This experience demonstrated to me once again that I shouldn't worry about the "how" so much when chanting, as long as the "what" was very clearly focused upon, in my mind. When we are focused on the "what", synchronicities begin to occur in our lives. In addition, this experience revealed to me another principle of which, until then, I had not been fully aware.

Once we have set an intention, it is essential to let it go and not to grasp and cling to it. It is only by letting go that it is possible for things to actually manifest. Once we release our grasp on that which we desire, we give up our resistance towards it and those things which we desire can come to us.

If we are struggling to achieve a goal because we are emotionally attached to it, and if we only rely upon our own willpower alone, we will only close ourselves to the support of cosmic consciousness.

Exercise

How can you tell if you are opening up to cosmic consciousness? Have you ever experienced any of the following during or after chanting Daimoku?

☐ I discovered the right information at the right time.

☐ I felt an increased sense of joy and lightness.

☐ I noticed new ideas popping into my head.

☐ I experienced a miracle or synchronicity.

☐ I got guidance from someone or something outside of me.

☐ I received sudden insights into a long-standing problem.

☐ etc.

Chapter 10
Where is our focus?

> The key to success is to focus our conscious mind on things we
> desire not things we fear.   – Brian Tracy

What is our attention focused on?

Let´s go back to the dual aspect of the material world. The dual
aspect of wave-energy and physical particle, which is one of the
fundamental discoveries of quantum physics, indicates an astonishing fact. Basically, it's quite simple: energy waves become physical particles simply through observation:

A particular thing appears in our world
which we focus our attention on.

It was Dr. Gary E. Schwartz, the Director of the Laboratory for
Advances in Consciousness and Health in the Department of Psychology at the University of Arizona, who discovered that an intention produces a certain photon and electron arrangement.
This means we produce electromagnetic energy with our intentions which is determined not only by our conscious focus, i.e. to
that of which we are aware of and paying attention to, but also by
our subconscious mind. With special CCD cameras, Dr. Schwartz
has actually captured images of light emanating from people who
are sending positive thoughts to another person, e.g. a healing intention.

It is our focus which determines and creates our reality. Dr.
Schwartz has shown in his research that that which we focus on
increases in photon density – in other words – when our mind is
attentive to something, our attention rearranges photons at the
energetic level. Our intentions become actualized and manifest in

the physical world, as the photons and other subatomic particles arrange in accordance with our focused thought.

Our energy follows our attention. The universe reads our intentions by noticing our attention. When Buddha stated that "what you think you become", he was also teaching us the principle that what we intend and what we do will eventually return to us.

Whatever we focus on, we create a relationship with.

Exercise

Make a list of things you give your attention to every day.

_ _

What thoughts would you like to think and transmit to new networks in your brain? (e.g. Everything is possible. Great things are going to happen to me. Today will be a great day. I am amazed at what I can do. Life is so beautiful.)

_ _

Try to put all your attention on those thoughts and think them again and again.

_ _

What particular things will you do today in order to fulfil your aspirations and desires?

_ _

Mentally rehearse each particular action and thing as often as you can.

_ _

By mentally rehearsing new thoughts again and again, we slowly build up new neurological pathways and circuits in our brain. In other words, we are installing new software in our head. These thoughts will become a new, powerfully insistent voice in our head, drowning out all those disempowering negative thoughts from our past.

Consciousness is energy

From a scientific perspective, our intentions create new synaptic connections and neural circuits in our brains via neuroplasticity, which then emit frequencies based on electrical conductivity of action potentials.

Every creative act begins with thought – whether our new house, our new relationship or our next professional project. When we intend to do something, a complex chain of events begins in our brain. Thoughts glide across the neural pathways. As neurons fire together, they link up and generate electromagnetic fields. These fields are invisible energies, but recent research demonstrates that they affect and condition the material molecules around us. For, consciousness creates.

Medical researcher Dawson Church claims that projected intentions will lead to material creations. If an intention is especially focused and strong, he claims that the desired changes can be observed in the form of a synchronicity. Intention creates electromagnetic fields that determine the nature of our material world by affecting and conditioning the matter molecules around us.

The energy we generate determines the nature of our material reality. Our intentions create the world around us.

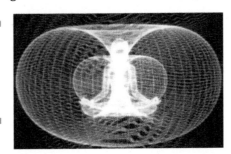

According to Dr. Michele Kattke, intention is a universal creative force which generates an energetic imprint that is an expression of consciousness. She claims that the energy frequency signature generated by an intention or thought interacts with the quantum field via interconnected quantum-holographic networks. This interaction links a mind and the universe as a whole, thereby attracting matching frequencies across space time through a process of magnetic gravitation.

Intention interacts with the quantum field,
thereby creating an electromagnetic energy field which will attract matching frequencies.

This is exactly what Nichiren had discovered more than 750 years ago. He tells us that our prayers will be answered like an echo. In other words, he teaches us that the energy of our thoughts, emotions, words and actions will attract similar energies into our life.

Exercise

What does the vibration of your electromagnetic energy match with?

- -

Does it match with what you already know?

- -

Does it match with new, unknown, exciting experiences?

- -

Where are we putting our attention?

Let's say we want to become an abundant person. In such a case, it is important to be aware of how much energy and focus is taken away from us simply by being anxious about money. For being anxious about money will not make us rich. Instead, try to focus on the feeling of having enough money while chanting, or on having a good job or on what you could do to have sufficient money in our life, so we need not worry about it anymore. It is who we are becoming in that process which matters most.

But what if we nevertheless frequently feel unworthy or afraid of not having sufficient money? We need to focus on our goal every day while chanting in order to get beyond thoughts and feelings such as "I can´t", or "it is too hard". Thoughts like "I will never be wealthy" or "money is bad" may still arise. Every day we need to get beyond thoughts and feelings of living in lack and being afraid to spend money. In this process, all our emotions of unworthiness and fear may still arise.

This is where the power of Daimoku functions most powerfully as a "pattern breaker," a matter we explored in the last chapter of our previous book »change your brainwaves - change your karma. Nichiren Buddhism 3.1«.

If each day we create a feeling of worthiness and abundance while chanting, then we are changing our life from the inside out, which will then be reflected in our environment. For we cannot achieve any of our goals without proper focus.

Exercise

Are you 100% willing to commit to achieving your goals?

_____

Are you willing to do whatever it takes to achieve your goal?

_____

Are you feeling you lack focus? Do you easily get distracted?

_____

Get a clear focus whilst chanting and in everyday life:

Start to focus deeply on your vision while chanting.

Stop distracting yourself. Begin to get rid of people, projects and things that do not help you to accomplish your vision.

Matter and consciousness are not separate

Our state of consciousness is in resonance with the circumstances, occasions and states of our own life. Only when we cultivate within ourselves a clear state of consciousness with a focused intention towards a particular situation, then our inner state will be reflected in the circumstances of our external world.

If we want to change our reality, then
the first change begins with our consciousness.

If we want to be successful, for example, by starting a business, then it is important to build up a feeling of success, which means to cultivate a positive attitude towards successful people. If we want to be healthy, it is necessary to develop a vital health awareness and to focus on being healthy. If we want to have happy relationships, then we need to show real appreciation to other people. By doing so, the quality of our consciousness can be compared to a filter, through which we are able to create or properly perceive the external circumstances of our lives. Crucial to our lives, whether experienced in love and happiness or in disease, suffering and conflict, is ultimately the nature of our consciousness. With reference to our own particular lives, this normally means: We always think that once we change our circumstances we will be able to enjoy a good life. Yet the observer effect tells us that actually the opposite is true: We must be happy first, and then our outer world will be transformed. If we change the focus of our attention, then our external circumstances begin to change. Of course, our external circumstances might still remain the same on the surface. Maybe we don´t have the money right now to go on that trip to the Caribbean, maybe we don´t have the time. Then we are more tuned into the frequency of our immediate problems and current circumstances, rather than the liberating frequency of our dreams and positive aspirations.

> Never let your current reality define your actuality!

Most significantly, Daisaku Ikeda tells us that we must always resonate with the frequency of our dreams rather than the frequency of our current circumstances and limitations.

> "What kind of future do I envision for myself? What kind of self am I trying to develop? What do I want to accomplish in my life?"
>
> The thing is to paint this vision of your life in your heart as specifically as possible. That "painting" itself becomes the design of your future.
>
> The power of the heart enables us to actually create with our lives a wonderful masterpiece in accordance with that design.

He does not want us to tell the Gohonzon how big and unsolvable our problems are but rather to tell our problems and circumstances how big the Gohonzon is. He tells us that the source of our greatest abundance and wealth is this invisible creative process within us when we become co-creators with the universal power of Nam-myō-hō ren-ge-kyō. However, we still need a clear, positive vision, aspiration or intention in order that our prayer will be effective. Consequently, I have asked myself for a long time:

what actually is an intention? We will explore this further in the chapters which follow.

Chapter 11
Myō-Hō in action: the power of intention

> The invisible is always the origin of the visible. — *William Tiller*

The power of the invisible

The term *Myō-Hō* signifies the dual aspect of potentiality and actuality. In order to activate this reality creating mechanism, prayer is required. A prayer in Nichiren Buddhism is chanting Daimoku accompanied by a specific intention or vision. Our intentions create what is  envisioned in the invisible spiritual realm first. This is the essential first step to manifesting our desires in the visible realm.

So understood, our intentions and visualizations are represented by the character "Myō", which more generally represents the invisible realm itself. Accordingly, the actual manifestation of our intentions and visualizations is represented by the character "Hō", which more generally represents actual manifestation in the material visible realm itself. Clearly, we must first "envision" our new reality in order that it manifest in the visible realm.

Myō= Intention, Hō = Manifestation

As considered above, behind every material form we perceive that there is a non-material, energetic dimension. Each material form has its energetic counterpart. They belong together like the two sides of a coin. The process of bringing something from out of a state of potentiality into a present state of manifestation requires an essential component: our own observation, which means our intention.

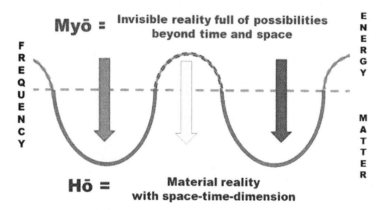

Manifestation of Intentions

Myō = **Invisible reality full of possibilities beyond time and space**

F R E Q U E N C Y

E N E R G Y

M A T T E R

Hō = **Material reality with space-time-dimension**

Only our observation, which means our expectation and intention, can activate the reality-creating function of "Myō-Hō" through chanting.

So we need to have a clear idea about that which we want to achieve. If we focus on what we want to achieve while chanting, will it then manifest in actuality? A proper understanding of the principle of Myō-Hō helps us to realize that we actually manifest from the world of the unseen or invisible into the present material world.

Such new ideas may sound strange, as we still tend to habitually think just as people have thought over the past few centuries. For it radically undermines our ordinary understanding of reality when it is said that the reality of things "at their deepest core" has much more to do with our own consciousness than we usually think. The German quantum physicist, Prof. Hans Peter Dürr (1929-2014), outlined one of the most fundamental discoveries resulting from research in quantum physics as follows:

> If we keep taking matter apart, there will ultimately be nothing left that reminds us of matter. In the end there is no longer any matter, but only shape, form, symmetry, relationship. Matter is not composed of matter! Basically, there remains only something that is more like the spiritual - holistic, open, lively, potentiality. [...] It is real creation: turning potential into reality.
>
> — *Hans Peter Dürr*

Consequently, behind the visible reality Prof. Dürr assumed a hidden invisible immaterial dimension which he called the "force of action (Wirkkraft)." Further, this spiritual power can be understood as the power of consciousness itself.

Susanne talking with Prof. Hans-Peter Dürr about Buddhism and Quantum physics in Heidelberg, 2013

For he definitely thought that material reality is not something independent of our own consciousness, and over which we have no influence or control, but rather that our mind itself does have significant influence on our immediate reality. He highlighted this as follows:

> Reality is not a fixed reality out there, it is full of possibilities outside and in each of us. They can be modified or redesigned by each of us. If we all maintain a vision of this far more open reality, found both within and in front of each of us, then finally we will succeed in becoming aware of a far more vibrant world.
>
> Ibid.

According to Prof. Dürr, it would seem that consciousness is more fundamental than matter. It would also seem that focused energy or intent has a significant, measurable impact on both people and material objects. Perhaps we need to rethink the very nature of matter itself. All matter may well be consciousness. Do we exist in an intersection between the physical and the spiritual, where focused intention can itself impact on and affect material reality in a measurable and visually perceptible way?

Does consciousness affect physical reality?

Could it be that our consciousness has a far more profound influence on the circumstances of our lives than we ordinarily imagine and that in fact we shape our present reality with our thoughts and our consciousness? That's a question which several scientists also asked themselves near the end of the last century.

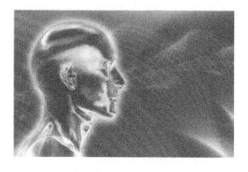

With the aim of investigating the "role of consciousness in creating physical reality", a research program was launched in 1979 under the direction of Robert G. Jahn and his colleague Brenda Dunne from Princeton University in the US to find out whether human consciousness is able to influence physical reality. For the observer effect provided strong evidence that attention alone could influence matter.

Consequently, the researchers asked themselves whether a very definite focused intention was even more able to influence matter. What in fact can thoughts affect and are thoughts actually able to influence mere material processes? How much power does a thought have? They really wanted to find all this out. To this end, intention was defined as very definite goal-oriented action.

In contrast to a mere wish, intension is particularly characterized by a highly-motivated, goal-oriented mode of thinking and acting.

Mental influence on electronic devices

In their PEAR laboratory ("Princeton Engineering Anomalous Research"), for over 25 years, the researchers examined the effects of the human mind on inanimate objects, such as random generators and electronic devices. Their aim was to discover whether consciousness is able to influence machine-controlled processes. Let's give an example. Subjects were placed in front of a screen and instructed to attempt to influence an electronic device in such a way that one of two pictures, for instance, would appear more

often. The devices were activated at random and each presented alternating pictures of Indians and cowboys (in proportion: 50-50). The participants had then to attempt to influence the device so that it presented images of either Indians or cowboys more frequently. In this case, they focused on making the Indian image appear more frequently. The results were remarkable. Human intention was actually able to influence the electronic devices in the desired direction.

After 2.5 million controlled experiments, the research group came to the definite conclusion that human intention alone was able to influence an electronic device in such a way as to attain the desired outcome. The researchers had evidence that human consciousness can directly affect physical reality. They concluded that:

> Consciousness and physical reality interact with each other
> naturally as our consciousness itself ultimately consists of energy
> in its finest and most dynamic form.

Distant mental influence on another person

In turn, other researchers focused on investigating how thoughts can affect other living beings. In this context, the American psychologist William Braud (1942-2012) demonstrated that human thought can influence the direction in which fish swim. He was also able to demonstrate that a person could have a direct mental influence on someone else's autonomic nervous system. His investigations demonstrated that someone who is being stared at reacts subconsciously. He discovered this by measuring the skin resistance and thus the stress level of the person concerned, while they were being stared at.

William Braud also investigated whether our positive thoughts can have an effect on other people. Can we use our positive intentions to help other people? Using measurements with biofeedback devices, the researchers found that the good intentions of another person can be just as effective for us as our good intentions for ourselves. Further research demonstrated that we can most powerfully and positively influence others to be more "orderly" if we ourselves are harmonious, which implies inner coherence. The calmer we ourselves are, the more we are able to calm mentally distressed people. The better we can concentrate and attain coherence ourselves, the better the people around us can concentrate and attain coherence.

Animals can influence a robot

Other studies have even discovered that animals are also able to use their intentions effectively. Scientist René Peoch from France wanted to know if the mental activity of a chick could influence the movement of a mobile robot that the chick considered to be its "mother hen", but was in fact controlled by a computer program for a random generator.

After allowing the robot to run randomly in an enclosed area, a chick was put into a cage. The robot then began to move (measured at almost 80%) more frequently towards the chick cheeping in the cage. The cheeping chick had apparently expressed a clear "intention" that her "mother hen" come close to her. If such a small animal's intention is quite sufficient to have such a significant impact on a robot, how much stronger must the effect of human intention be?

The path of the random event generator in the experiments with a chick

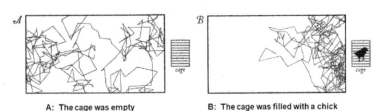

A: The cage was empty   B: The cage was filled with a chick
                                            imprinted on the robot

The sophisticated experiments which scientists have carried out in this subject area suggests that the mind or human consciousness appears to be inextricably linked to matter. Human consciousness is able to influence and change material reality. Recent research has also demonstrated, that living beings constantly send out and receive energy.

Your own intention acts like a tuning fork that causes other things in your environment to resonate at the same frequency.

- Lynne McTaggart

Chapter 12
What is on our mind?

| Intention is a process of creation. | — *William Tiller* |

Daimoku amplifies our intentions

In our previous book "Transform your energy-change your life-Nichiren Buddhism 3.0" we argued that biophotons are essential to increase the energy field around your body. How much energy you have, seems to be directly related to the effect of the intentions you send out. For Dr. Gary Schwartz demonstrated that biophotons appear to have a decisive impact when it comes to increasing the power of our intentions. His research implies that human intention is a living creative force which has an impact through the emission of light particles (biophotons).

Professor Fritz Albert Popp considers biophotons to be an energy life force that transmits information within our bodies. If an intention has an effect through the emission of biophotons, then whatever we set our mind on in order to achieve it implies that a part of our life force is transmitted to that particular goal or vision. In fact, the intensity of our desire seems directly proportional to the power of our focused intentions.

If we do not have a clear goal or vision or definite objective, then we are more likely to tune in to all the other streams of light particles generated by the intentions and visions of those people in our environment. The intentions of other people will energetically assert themselves against our own intentions thereby hindering the manifestation of our own particular visions. Consequently, in this respect, it is better to speak of our "determination" in realizing our particular visions, as the intensity of our determination is characterized by a high-density energy which carries out our intentions.

In fact, a direct intention manifests itself as electric and magnetic energy which leads to an ordered emission of photons. Our intentions appear to function as highly coherent frequency patterns which are even capable of changing the molecular structure of matter itself. As chanting Daimoku energetically increases the number and intensity of biophotons we emit; and as our focused intention in fact manifests itself as an emission of such light particles; clearly, the chanting of Daimoku acts as an amplifier of our intentions. This is something which I had always been aware of since I began chanting Daimoku. Nichiren himself described this phenomenon like this:

> There is in the entire world no place where the sound of chanting Daimoku can't reach. Even though our voice is weak and low, Daimoku amplifies it to a loud sound and carries it into all the places of the great sphere of 3,000 worlds. It sounds like you blow your weak voice into a shell that carries a loud sound far away [...]. This is the important doctrine of *Ichinen Sanzen*.
>
> From *Nikō's Records* of Nichiren's lectures
> on the Lotus Sutra held at Minobu between 1278 and 1280

Daimoku is an amplifier and carrier which transmits our intentions
to the entire universe. Later, the echo of our Daimoku returns
to us from all places and all times.

Nichiren teaches us that our prayers will be answered like an echo that follows a sound. This means if the sound is weak, scattered or incoherent, the echo will also be weak, scattered or incoherent. In the same way, our intention can be strong or weak. When we constantly doubt whether our intention will have an effect or when we are thinking about what we do not want instead of what we want, our intention will only lead to a weak and incoherent result. Consequently, the more coherent, clear and strong our intention is, the more coherent, clear and strong will be the result and effect in our life.

> Intention has a central, forceful role in creating reality and is a potent energy capable of influencing and transforming the material, tangible world.

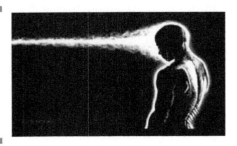

The power of what we think each day

Many people think that our intention in the context of chanting is simply a powerful thought which we have only while chanting twice a day. We chant in the morning and we focus on our intention for that day. In the evening we focus once again on our goals and what we want to achieve in life. And we may be tempted to think that this is the only thing which the universe actually hears.

However, we tend to forget the things we have been thinking about, usually unconsciously, all day. I have had many questions from people who have asked me why their hopes and intentions focused upon while chanting have not as yet come about. A middle-aged woman, for example, used to complain to me: "I chant a lot every morning and evening, but I have not managed to get a new job yet". In this particular case, I was aware of a tendency which hindered her. She was very pessimistic about being able to get a new job, as she was constantly thinking that she was just too old to get a new job. I wondered, whether these negative thoughts were deeply impacting on and affecting the outcome of her chanting Daimoku.

However, sometimes the exact opposite occurs. I have often asked myself why it is that even though I have not been consciously chanting for a particular outcome, sometimes an unconscious wish or desire I have had in my mind nevertheless comes about in a synchronistic and usually surprising manner?

Case study 11: What are you thinking about?

I experienced this several years ago when I suddenly got a call from the secretary of the German Buddhist Union, which at that time I had been serving as a council member. I was told that I had been referred to the director of a newly established scientific magazine, as he was looking for someone to write an article on Buddhism and quantum physics. This topic was one of my main interests at that time, so I contacted him and told him my ideas on the subject. He was very pleased to publish my article in his magazine. After the magazine had come out, he called me to tell me that my article had been rated as the most interesting article by readers. I was really surprised.

At that moment I became aware that for the last couple of months I had frequently been thinking to myself that I would love to publish an article in a magazine, writing about spirituality and science. And now this had come about.

I had the feeling that this experience had very much to do with the expanding of my consciousness while chanting. I realized that what I think and feel throughout each day is also an intention which "is noticed" by cosmic consciousness and thereby has an enormous impact on my life.

Can our thoughts travel into the future and shape our life? There is scientific evidence implying that our present intentions can influence what events actually will come into being. As described in previous chapters, reality is not rigidly fixed but highly mutable, and consequently very much open to influence, and we are central to the entire process as powerful influencers.

So can our thoughts and intentions in daily life act as a positive, impactful energy which might be capable of changing our environment, heal each other or to powerfully affect and transform matter?

> Be vigilant, guard your mind against negative thoughts.
> —*Buddha*

We experience what is on our mind

I would never have thought that our thoughts, judgments, wishes and intentions were actually something "real" which could physically affect not only myself but also my environment. However, in the course of many years, I have noticed a curious phenomenon often experienced by those who chant Daimoku. I realized that they tended to experience exactly what is on their mind, what they have been feeling and thinking about for the past weeks, months or even years.

To give a concrete example, one woman always wondered if her marriage was still working and she thought about getting a divorce. A few months later, her husband had an affair and left her. She ended up getting a divorce. When this happened, she was actually devastated and heartbroken. Yet it occurred to me that this was exactly what had been on her mind for a long time. It was as if her thoughts had become reality.

Similar things also happened to people who had positive thoughts and hopes in their minds throughout each day. Another woman kept talking about changing her job and began studying. This was against all the odds, as she was a forty-year-old single mother with an immigrant background and had been working for the last twenty years as a hairdresser. Further, the statistical chance of being admitted to university was less than 10 percent. Nevertheless, despite these challenging circumstances, she regularly saw herself walking in and out of the university building whenever she walked past its entrance. She kept on chanting to be admitted to this particular university which she was always imagining in her mind and eventually she succeeded.

We described the experience of this Turkish woman in chapter 7 of our book »Transform your energy – Change your life: Nichiren

Buddhism 3.0«. Subsequently, four years later, she successfully completed her studies and this year began to work as a social worker employed by the city administration. As it turned out, she was really fortunate to get the job at that particular time. She began to work on the first of March this year and exactly three weeks later the Corona virus crisis flared up. She would never have been hired a month later as companies and local authorities were in lockdown. Nor would she have been able to continue to work as a hairdresser as all hairdressing-shops were likewise closed down. She only realized later how lucky she had been.

Another woman chanted for a particular job she hoped to get. She was very specific in her intentions while chanting. She wanted to earn a particular amount of money, have nice colleagues and meaningful work to do, as up to now she had been working for a forwarding agency, doing work which she did not consider to be very meaningful. However, she began to get desperate about finding her hoped for job and she made several job applications. The next day she was invited for a job interview and it turned out that the job she was offered met all the specific criteria she had been chanting for. The job was offered to her by a company that produced software for psychologists. She considered it to be very valuable and meaningful to work to support psychologists. So she accepted the job and began working a week later.

All the experiences described above made me realize that not only our conscious and but also our unconscious thoughts about our circumstances and other people profoundly affect our current relationships and everyday world.

Our mind can literally shape our destiny.
Thoughts are so powerful that they even have an immediate impact on our physical body.

Our thoughts are constantly being transmitted

Generally, we are brought up to believe that our thoughts simply belong to our inner world alone. I always used to think, that whatever I had been thinking throughout the day, how I had been secretly judging people, whatever I had been wishing for myself and all my many intentions and hopes were just taking place inside my head and were therefore completely inaccessible to other people. I would have never thought that others might be able to know what I am thinking. Yet the more I chanted Daimoku, the more I became aware that I could often sense what other people were actually feeling and thinking. I also realized that my thoughts and my feelings are not just locked up inside my brain or my body. Other people could sense them, too.

I experienced this once again the other day when I did a little test on my husband. We were in a restaurant waiting for the food to be served. I used this time to find out whether he could actually read my thoughts. I told him I would be focusing my thoughts on an object that was especially important to me and he should try to discover what it was. I closed my eyes and visualized with great intensity my mother's golden bracelet which she had worn throughout her life. I was wondering whether my husband could sense or "see" the bracelet I was thinking about. He knew that I was thinking about an object which he was supposed to discover. After a while he said that it was strange but that an image of my mother kept coming to his mind and that he felt compelled to think about my mother. I almost cringed. I had been thinking about my mother's bracelet and my husband had completely picked up on the emotional content of what I had been thinking about. He had also picked up on a certain information and its emotional content from the past, as my mother had died a long time ago and my husband has never actually met her.

Exercise

Just try this test with a friend and find out if your friend can tell you what you are thinking right now. What was the result?

Our thoughts are contagious

We frequently think that we are just sending out our power thoughts, hopes and particular intentions only when chanting in the morning and evening. Yet in actuality, we are transmitting our intentions throughout each day. We are both transmitting and receiving information at each moment. Our transmissions are being registered and responded to. For we are all part of an interconnected psychic network. But what does that really mean? Well, it is very simple. It means that our thoughts and emotions are highly contagious.

So what are we transmitting to the people in our life? For example, what is it that you have been thinking about those people in your life who never seem to make any progress? About a daughter who never tidies up her room? Or a husband who never helps with the dishes? Are we frustrated? And what are we transmitting because of our frustration? What are we secretly thinking about our boss? We tend to think that thoughts are locked inside our heads, yet they nevertheless find their way into the consciousness of other people. We think that our innermost feelings and thoughts will remain unknown to other people. Yet it would seem that we are all intimately connected on the psychic, intuitive level. In fact, our thoughts and feelings are read and known by others. Do we wonder why we are not getting a lot of recognition at work, yet our colleague does? Is not the real question about what are our inner feelings and thoughts about our boss and the job? Our boss might have registered our inner resentment and criticism of him on the unspoken, energetic level. The real issue is what are the secret thoughts and judgements we make about other people in our environment. Such secret thoughts frequently manifest in the behavior of people around us.

Our thoughts are being transmitted to other people.

Exercise

Write down your thoughts about the people closest to you in your immediate environment. What are your secret thoughts about them?

_____

Imagine another person knows what your inner feelings and thoughts are. How would you react if you were them?

_____

Can you feel a change in a person's behavior or in the situation in general when you chant for this particular person's happiness?

_____

Do your own intention experiment. Focus on the fulfillment of your friend's goals and desires while chanting. Notice whether she or he begins to behave in a different way towards you.

_____

Chapter 13

The power of focused intention

Prayer is a form of intentional magic, a mental act intended to affect the world in some way.
— *Dean Radin*

Our own consciousness is part of cosmic consciousness

Just imagine the universe as a vast ocean of consciousness, in which we are part of and connected with everything else, just as Nichiren describes it:

It is called the Mystic Law because it reveals the principle of the mutually inclusive relationship of a "single moment of life" [a heart] and all phenomena. [...] Life at each moment encompasses all phenomena and permeates their entire realm.
On Attaining Buddhahood in This Lifetime, WND I: 3

Our capacity for having a specific intention comprises a very significant part of this consciousness. Science today tells us that it is our intention which has an infinite coordinating function within this vast ocean of consciousness. It has been discovered that our deliberate intentions can make our visions manifest as reality and we can thereby achieve things beyond the ordinary.

In the past decade, this topic has drawn increasing attention from researchers. It is now being asked: what is an intention? What determines its strength and its effects? Many believe that a thought or an intention is in fact a tangible energy which can have a direct physical impact on events, as well as on living and non-living things.

There are scientists who say that
human intention exists in physical form.

Among such scientists is Dr. William Tiller, professor emeritus of physics at Stanford University, who wanted *to find out whether our conscious intention can influence the material world.* He investigated what consciousness *is* by asking in a basic way what consciousness *does.* Our consciousness does things through intentionality. Dr. Tiller considers that having a clear, focused intention requires a steady mind. Then the effects of intention can be quite astonishing. What he discovered is indeed groundbreaking.

The participants in his studies were asked to focus on specific things and send a particular intention to water. For example, the participants were asked to seek to intentionally raise or lower the acidity (Ph) of water, or to raise the activity of a particular liver enzyme. They were also asked to attempt  to change the ATP (adenosine triphosphate) production in fruit fly larvae, so enabling them to mature more quickly. The results were astonishing.

By way of focused intention, the participants actually did raise or lower the Ph of water by one unit and raise the activity of the liver enzyme by 30%. They also succeeded in making the fruit larvae mature more quickly. The recorded results were highly significant, as the statistical possibility of chance occurrence was less than one in 1000.

Human intention imprints the space around it

Further, Tiller's experiments led to another significant discovery. The participant's minds were able to influence things more effectively and quickly the more frequently the experiments were repeated. The environment in which the experiments were conducted appeared to be conditioned by the minds of the participants. The same would also appear to apply to the environment or locations in which healing takes place.

Human consciousness actually conditions or
"imprints" empty space.

Dr. Tiller considers that this phenomenon demonstrates that intensively repetitive acts of intention will enhance the amount of electrical "charge" and activates a kind of a coherence or organizing principle, i.e. a coherence which will change the material thermodynamic processes of a particular location. Indeed, such coherence tended to increase the more the act of intention was repeated. For it is such states of coherence that make our intentions especially strong.

> As long as the intended change is visualized clearly, the belief is strong and the emotional force behind the intention is both focused and sustained, your intention can change your environment.   — William Tiller.

This also explains why chanting Daimoku seems to act as an amplifier of the information content and energy of our thoughts and feelings we are projecting out into the universal consciousness. Our findings with respect to brain wave measurements similarly indicate that this is the case, as we would appear to enter a notably coherent brainwave state when chanting.

Further, with respect to Dr. Tiller's findings, one might say that the more coherent our brain is when chanting and sending out an intention, the more energy we have to affect and imprint the environment around us or to wherever we are projecting our intentions. In fact, the effect is like that of a laser, where waves of an ambient field will become more ordered. For an intention would appear to ripple through ambient space like an intense, precisely targeted beam of light. Thus, Tiller's research seems evidence for the suggestion that we should consider intentionality as one of the primary factors affecting our personal lives and the lives of others.

> For the last four hundred years, an unstated assumption of science is that human intention cannot affect what we call „physical reality". Our experimental research of the past decade shows that, for today's world and under the right conditions, this assumption is no longer correct.   – *William Tiller*

Just imagine what this means for the environment we live or work in. For intention can also be negative. When we have constant arguments at home or feel anger towards our colleagues and boss, we may also influence the physical space of our home and our office and anyone who later stays in this environment is more likely to be frustrated or angry. The same happens when we send out love and appreciation towards the people we live and work with. We positively condition the environment around us and live more harmoniously together.

Tiller's work demonstrates that we should appreciate how crucial our attitudes of mind are when performing our daily tasks.

The power of a sacred space

The concept of a "conditioned space" was first explored by former Princeton psychologist Dr. Roger Nelson, whose professional focus was the study of intention and the role of the mind in the physical world. Among other things, he investigated whether there was a special "charge" to particular places that were generally considered to be "sacred sites". After some experiments, he came to the conclusion that these places contained a "field consciousness" which contained a high volume of coherent energy. For, positive intentions and acts of praying seem to condition a space and make its energy more vital and coherent.

I experienced such a vibrant, positive and clear energy when we followed in Nichiren's footsteps to Mount Minobu. After climbing a steep path through the forest we passed the

place where Nichiren had lived in his hut between May 1274 and November 1281. Standing before this particular place, I was deeply moved. I reflected on all the Daimoku he would have recited at this particular place, and how his original vow and intention and the energy of his perpetual prayer must still be "stored" here. I could feel the original "conditioning" of this sacred space and the dynamic energy of Nichiren's Daimoku. And indeed, there is an exceptionally strong energy which envelops this place and grabs you. It just cannot be resisted.

If one continues further up and climbs some more steep steps, one finally reaches Nichiren's grave. A couple of meters in front of it, there is a small wooden construction where one can chant Daimoku or recite Gongyo. When I chanted before Nichiren's grave, I suddenly felt myself being

Nichiren's grave in Minobu

transported to a radically different dimension. I felt myself to be in an ethereal sphere, characterized by an enchanting, exquisite

Chanting Daimoku in front of Nichiren's grave in Minobu

fragrance. I felt as if I was no longer on this coarse earth. It was the most blissful and secure feeling I have ever enjoyed.

In the same way, we condition the environment around our own Gohonzon, the place where we chant Daimoku every day. I can always feel the different atmosphere in a place where lots of Daimoku have been chanted. There is an elevated, uplifting energy which remains for quite some time. In such a way, we create our own "sacred space" surrounding our butsudan, i.e. our altar. This is further confirmation of the principle that Nichiren outlined when he was speaking of the place where we chant Daimoku is indeed the sacred place of enlightenment:

> In the Latter Day of the Law, no treasure tower exists other than the figures of the men and women who embrace the Lotus Sutra. [...] Abutsubō, you yourself are a Tathāgata who is originally enlightened and endowed with the three bodies of a Buddha. You should chant Nam-myoho-renge-kyo with this conviction. Then the place where you chant Daimoku will become the dwelling place of the treasure tower. Chapter 11 of the Lotus Sutra reads, "If there is any place where the Lotus Sutra is

> preached, then my treasure tower will come forth and appear in that spot."
>
> *On the Treasure Tower (To the Honorable Abutsubō),*
> WND I: 299 f.

The place before the Mandala Gohonzon where we sit and chant Daimoku is sacred as it is thereby transformed into the very place where the Ceremony in the Air eternally takes place.

The contagious power of intention

It is important to remember that "thought and feeling" are equivalent to "intention", although there is a difference in effect between "ordinary thoughts" and those thoughts which arise from a state of focused meditation, resulting in a clearly intended outcome or particular state. This implies that intention affects every aspect of our life. This is particularly relevant when considering negative thoughts and feelings, such as feelings of low self-worth and self-depreciation or negative intentions generally towards other people and things. For each of these have clear consequences, both for the one projecting their intentions and for those to whom those intentions are directed.

Tiller's findings have demonstrated that for any intention to be effective it must be focused and coherent.

Human intentions appear to have a contagious power which affects the world.

Does this mean that we can use our intention to affect the outcome of a medical treatment, make our business grow more quickly or even solve an international conflict? Nichiren taught us that we can do all of this if we combine our intention with the power of Daimoku. Didn't he tell Shijō Kingo that chanting Daimoku with the intention of healing his daughter could indeed heal her? Further, Nichiren told him to chant with the intention of overcoming his problems with his "boss". And sure enough, Shijō Kingo solved his problems and ended up getting twice as much land as he had before after reconciling with his landlord. He clearly states that our hopes and intentions will become true if we chant Daimoku. All this requires a lot of stamina, as Dr. Tiller's research has shown, because intention affects and imprints the space in the environment on which an intention is focused. This can take time. We might ask ourselves why it is that sometimes people do not achieve what they want, despite the fact that they have chanted for it for a long time. Yet in order to actualize our intentions, we need to develop a dynamic energy by repeated practice and not become disheartened at the first or second setback. Overcoming tough times or setbacks through persistent practice is the only true path to success.

The rebound effect of chanting for others

Probably, we all know from experience that any type of altruistic act is beneficial not only for other people but also for ourselves. In fact, Nichiren explains this principle as being quite a natural phenomenon:

If you give alms to others, you will also be helped, just as, for example, if you hold a light for others, it will brighten your own way as well.

The Three Virtues of Food, WND II: 1060

We should keep in mind that intention affects everything, not only the person to whom an intention is being sent to but also the person who projects his or her intentions.

I remember when I began chanting, that I often used to chant with another woman, whom I referred to above. She worked as a nurse and had overcome multiple sclerosis through chanting Daimoku. I have never forgotten the story she told me about how this happened.

Case study 12: Chanting for the health of other people

She had been in hospital and feeling really desperate about her situation. She would look for a quiet place where she could chant a lot in order to improve her circumstances. Then things got even worse. Besides her own poor health, one day she also received a message that her father had himself become seriously ill and was in hospital. That's when she started chanting exclusively to improve his health, whenever she could find the time and space to do so. She completely forgot about her own situation and just focused on sending a healing intention to her father while chanting. She chanted for him to completely overcome his illness and for him to be healthy and happy in future. After two weeks, something rather miraculous occurred. She herself had begun to get much better the moment she had begun to chant for someone else. Her multiple sclerosis went into complete remission and has never returned since. It seemed that a powerful force had been responsible for this seemingly miraculous cure: the rebound effect of chanting for other people.

There has been an interesting study by Dr. Sean O´Laoire, a clinical psychologist in transpersonal psychology, on the effects of praying for, and sending out healing intentions to others. The study has confirmed that sending out healing intentions to others may well have a hugely positive effect on the person sending out the intention. Originally, Dr. O'Laoire had planned to explore whether those who received a positive healing intention experienced any change in their health or in their psychological state, such as a positive change of mood from anxiety or depression. He recruited 90 volunteers who were instructed to make positive vis-ualizations and send healing intentions to 406 volunteer-recipi-ents, who were asked to record and write down any changes in their mood or health while receiving the intentions. The results were astonishing.

It was clear that the healing intentions had had a positive effect on the recipients. All 406 recipients recorded a significant im-provement in their physical and psychological health. Yet what was even more surprising, was that those sending out the healing intentions were doing considerably better than the ones who had received the intentions. This result was completely unexpected. Dr. O´Laoire concluded that it would seem that praying for others was more beneficial than being prayed for.

> Healing intentions have a mirror effect. They not only affect the recipient of our intentions but reflect back on us as well.

Practice for oneself and for others

I have always been fascinated by this phenomenon among mem-bers of SGI. Whenever someone in a local group is facing a serious health challenge, members just get together and chant for this person. The first time I experienced this (and every single time since), I have felt extremely uplifted and energized by chanting for other people. It sometimes seems to be the secret catalyst, if you have been chanting for your own goals for a long time and nothing seems to have changed. I realized that instead of becoming des-perate, it was far better to simply "detach from one's self" and to focus on chanting for the happiness and well-being of another person.

For focusing far too much on our own intention and goal can be like watching a pot which never boils. For chanting for others takes the focus away from ourselves for a period, which then al-lows things to flow more freely. It would seem that being of service to others and chanting for them is the secret of "letting go" and that *not* observing our own intentions for ourselves with too much rigor is a more certain way to guarantee a desired outcome.

When reflecting upon the rebound effect of chanting Daimoku for other people, however, we should not think that we help other people primarily for our own benefit. Research has shown that this rebound effect is primarily activated if we help selflessly without expecting anything in return. For Nichiren, it was simply a natural law that we help ourselves when helping others and that we can never be happy by seeking our own happiness alone. We will manifest the quality of a Bodhisattva of the Earth quite naturally if we continue to chant Daimoku. During this process we will develop more self-respect, as well as more compassion for others. At the same time, we will accumulate more good fortune to enrich our own life.

We are all living in a particular society, in a particular country and in this world together. Consequently, Nichiren appealed to the political authorities of his time to take measures to protect the country from natural disasters as well as from civil war and foreign invasion.

> If you lose your country because of a foreign invasion or your home due to natural catastrophe, then to where can you escape from this world? If you are sincerely concerned about your own security, you should first of all pray for peace and order throughout the four quarters of the land, should you not?
>
> *On Establishing the Correct Teaching*
> *for the Peace of the Land*, WND I: 24

Today, in our violent, disordered, globalized world, international peace and mutual understanding has become an urgent requirement, if our own security and happiness in this life is to be ensured. And this necessitates the propagation of the Mystic Law which should be realized deep within each one of us. In this

respect, we are also seeking to help others understand the profound and precious dignity of their own lives and the lives of all
others.

We contribute to world peace by praying
for it and for the welfare and happiness of all beings on earth.

Chapter 14
Determining on our own visions

Knowing what you want is the first step in getting it.

- Oprah Winfrey

Expressing our wish to enjoy a proactive and fulfilling life

If we could have absolutely anything in the world, including doing anything and being anything, what would that be? Imagine walking in a forest and all of a sudden a genie appears and asks: "I can immediately fulfill any wish you tell me! Just tell me, what is it that you want?" Would we know the answer straight away? Do we have a clear picture of what exactly that would look like? Or would we hesitate to give an answer as we have so many wishes and dreams that we would like to realize? Or would we give many reasons why our wish could never be realized? Whatever reason we come up with as to why fulfilling our dreams is impossible is an aspect of that restricting inner dialogue which keeps so many of us from ever envisioning what we really want. In such a case, we need to discover what our inner blockages are. Once we have done that, we need to make a determined effort to overcome them.

The question "What do you really want?" sounds quite simple, yet there are so many factors conditioning it, that it sometimes seems impossible to give a definite answer to it. We are normally over-involved in our stressful daily activities and need to detach in order to truly find ourselves. For this purpose, sitting down and chanting Daimoku in front of the Gohonzon is the best way to sincerely ask ourselves what we really want. After having discovered own particular answers, we can then begin to envision our future lives. For our reality will be a manifestation of those very visions.

It's all about living joyfully and mindfully every moment of each day. Living a life of abundance, having leisure time and exploring our interests. It's about enjoying time with our loved ones and experiencing adventure in our lives, too. It's about improving the quality of our lives. This also entails maintaining good health, physical fitness and emotional wellbeing, as well as experiencing uplifting emotions consistently and living harmoniously with the people you love. It also means financial security and pursuing a career which brings fulfillment and joy.

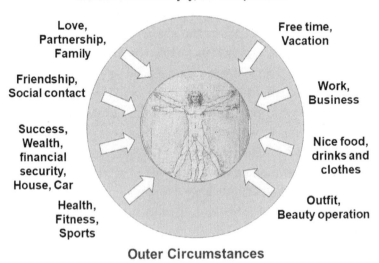

**A number of factors of happiness in daily life,
also in the form of joy, fun and pleasure**

Love,
Partnership,
Family

Free time,
Vacation

Friendship,
Social contact

Work,
Business

Success,
Wealth,
financial
security,
House, Car

Nice food,
drinks and
clothes

Health,
Fitness,
Sports

Outfit,
Beauty operation

Outer Circumstances

Such wishes reflect our desire to make our life enjoyable. That's why we spend so much of our energy, time and money on seeking to improve the external circumstances of our lives, such as professional career, family and personal relationships, money, health, and friendships.

Chanting Daimoku is the foundation for a happy life

However, although all these things are very important in order to enjoy a fulfilling life, they are largely things of external significance, things that have to do with our external environmental circumstances rather than things which can really make us happy in the long run. Nichiren considered that all these things relating to the outer circumstances of our lives are matters which can only bring us a transient, surface happiness. They only bring happiness on the surface, or on the secondary level, as they all ultimately depend on a much deeper sense of inner fulfillment and happiness, our primary happiness, without which we cannot enjoy any of the blessings in our lives. Each of these things in themselves are fragile and transient and they may swiftly perish or easily fall away.

As noted above in the section "Daimoku is the foundation of your daily life" in chapter 1, Nichiren advises us to consider our daily activities as in themselves a Buddhist practice. This means, that we should seek to fulfill our desires and enjoy life, yet always when centrally based on our Buddhist practice. This is because we may face difficulties in the process of realizing our goals and need strength and wisdom to overcome them. On the other hand, even if we could fulfill our desires, they could never become the foundation of a happy life. That's because our desires change, they are very fragile and ephemeral. They can only be well-grounded and enhanced by the unshakable foundation of our Buddhist practice.

> There is no true happiness for human beings other than chanting Nam-myoho-renge-kyo.
>
> *Happiness in this world*, WND I: 681

Chanting Daimoku keeps you directly linked to unlimited, non-local, cosmic consciousness, which is itself the source of "absolute happiness without reason," as it fills us with a deep lasting, fulfilling joy which is independent of events and things of our ordinary lives. Viewed from this perspective, we are each essentially good and endowed with all that is necessary to become fulfilled and happy. We don't need to demonstrate our personal value by what we have achieved or by what we represent to society. Instead, we should each regard everything in our lives as a process of self-development based on this deep conviction. Ultimately, it is not a question of WHAT WE HAVE or even what we have achieved. Such an unshakable foundation means that we can have trust and confidence that we are able to overcome all difficulties. Thus, Daisaku Ikeda encourages us:

> Despite what kind of situation or circumstances you find yourself in, the important thing is to not be defeated by your own timidity. A spring burgeoning with fortune and benefit will arrive for those who continue to advance with cheerful optimism no matter what befalls them.
>
> From "*To my friends*", published in the Seikyo Shimbun on February 28, 2020

The spiritual practice of chanting Daimoku before the Gohonzon serves as the foundation for a happy life
when we make sincere efforts to improve both our inner state and our outer circumstances.

Our secondary level of happiness

Having said that, it is nevertheless decisively important as to how we perceive and experience each area of our lives. None of them should be overlooked. For example, what good is it if we make a lot of money, but we have compromised our health in doing so? What good is being in great physical shape if our relationships are making us sad and unhappy? Further, without a solid financial background we can't even afford good medical treatment when we are sick or we can't enjoy a nice vacation to regain our strength. Thus, all aspects of our life are inter-connected and dependent on each other, something which cannot be ignored if our lives are to be pleasant and happy.

In order to ground a balanced life, it is also important for us to work on overcoming our own karmic tendencies as we struggle to achieve our life goals in our everyday social world. Let's say that we have set a goal to be successful in our professional career. That's when we would do best to learn all the required professional skills. However, we also need to enhance our social and communication skills with our colleagues, clients or customers. Throughout this whole process of learning and expanding our capacity, we face our karma, our particular patterns of thinking and behavior. Consequently, we need to deepen our Buddhist practice in order to resolve all difficulties and to overcome our karmic tendencies. This capacity becomes perhaps the greatest asset in our life.

We need to make a clear decision

Having a definite intention demands being clear about what we want. A true intention is a clear vision of about what we want. Let's say we want to be healed, we want a new job, or we  want a new relationship. We want to feel good. Or we are longing to live in a big city or to have a house at the seaside or in the countryside. At first, this is just a vague idea, but in order to have a clear vision, we need to be more specific, in the view of intention researcher Lynne McTaggart.

Let's take the new job, for example. Perhaps we ask ourselves what we need to earn per annum? Maybe we want to have three weeks vacation each year. This is to become more specific. We might tell ourselves: in this job, I would prefer to take a lot of business trips rather than working constantly in an office. I would like to work with supportive and stimulating people.

But the moment we ask ourselves further questions such as "what would it be like to have that new job?" we begin to create *a real vision* of that new job. When chanting, we should reflect on the word "job" or we should have a picture in our mind that is a vivid image unique to us. For such an image in our mind contains all of those factors which ensure that we have created a real, clear vision. And that vision is our actual *intention*. Once we see a clear picture of what we want while chanting, it begins to transform into a living motion picture, and we begin to make our dream an actuality.

Think big, free yourself from your present situation!
Be decisive! Create a clear picture in your mind for every area of your life! Visualize, chant and take action!

In order to create clear pictures in our minds for each area of our lives, we first have to find out what it is that we really want in respect of each area. This chapter will help us to ask ourselves what it is that we actually want. Most of us no longer ask ourselves this question anymore as we think the status quo of our life is a fixed-given which cannot be changed. Consequently, the first step to living a fulfilling life is to discover our real desires and to formulate our intentions. And we can best do this while chanting Daimoku in front of the Gohonzon.

Although there are probably many specific areas that are personally relevant to us, we have chosen to focus on the six most common areas which appear to be of particular significance to most people, that is: 1) our home and the way we live to meet our basic needs; 2) our health and wellness, which provides the basic foundation for an active life; 3) our romantic relationships, family and friendships, which provide emotional support; 4) our finances, especially our financial security ; 5) our professional career, which tends to occupy much of our time and energy, and is relevant to many other aspects of our lives, such as our particular abilities and capacity for personal development; and 6) the spiritual dimension, which provides the essential foundation for a fulfilled life.

Our next book, »Nichiren Buddhism 4.1«, will consider in more detail about how to develop a clear vision for each area of our lives in order to envision and create the life of which we dream when chanting. Consequently, our next book will be a blueprint to design the life we actually want. This requires asking ourselves detailed questions for each area of our lives, as it is only by this means that we arrive at a clear idea of what in fact it is that we really want. The questions below are designed to help us identify our particular intentions in each of the six areas of life considered above.

What would be your ideal home?

Exercise

What do you personally consider to be a nice home?

_ _ _ _ _ _ _ _ _ _ _ _ _ _ _

_ _ _ _ _ _ _ _ _ _ _ _ _ _ _

_ _ _ _ _ _ _ _ _ _ _ _ _ _ _

Are you satisfied with your current living arrangements? Do you live where you actually want to?

_ _

Do you live in the type of home that you actually desire?

_____

What type of home do you desire?

_____

Do you want to make any changes inside your home?

_____

What steps are you prepared to take in order to get your ideal home?

_____

Ask and answer any other question that you consider to be relevant to your home:

Q: _____

A: _____

My ideal home would be:

What would be your ideal state of health?

Exercise

What would it mean for you to live a healthy and active life?

_____

_____

How is your current health? Are you suffering from any medical conditions?

_____

Are you in the physical condition you would like to be in?

_____

Are you satisfied with the way that you take care of yourself?

_____

Are you as physically active as you would like to be?

_____

Are you happy with the way your body feels and looks?

_____

Do you smoke or eat too much processed food?

_____

Do you feel that you deserve to have a healthy body?

_____

Do you take time out to really relax?

_____

Do you have a clearly defined exercise program that you stick to?

_____

Are you on a healthy diet?

_____

How do you handle emotionally challenging situations?

_____

What changes would you like to make in respect of your physical and psychological health?

_____

How much are you prepared to do in order to make your vision come true?

_____

Ask yourself any other relevant question with respect to your health, if you have one:

Q: _____

A: _____

My vision concerning my health is:

What do you want in your emotional life?

This section considers three areas of your emotional life: your love relationships, your family and friendships, although of course these areas often overlap and cannot be sharply separated from each other.

1) love relationships

Exercise

What does it mean for you to enjoy a fulfilling relationship with a partner based on mutual love and respect?

_ _ _ _ _ _ _ _ _ _ _ _ _ _ _ _ _ _ _ _

_ _ _ _ _ _ _ _ _ _ _ _ _ _ _ _ _ _ _ _

_ _ _ _ _ _ _ _ _ _ _ _ _ _ _ _ _ _ _ _

If you are single and live alone, what kind of partner would you like to share your life with?

_ _

If you are currently in a relationship, are you happy with it?

_ _

Is your relationship fulfilling your emotional needs?

_ _

Are you concerned that you are in a toxic relationship that undermines you rather than inspires you?

_ _

What kind of relationship would you really want?

_____

A stable, well-grounded relationship that you can rely on?

_____

What would you do or become in order to find such a partner?

_____

What is it that you are essentially seeking in a relationship?

_____

What would you need to develop in yourself in order to be in such a relationship?

_____

Ask yourself any other relevant question with respect to your relationships, if you have one:

Q: _____

A: _____

My ideal relationship would be:

2) Family

Exercise

From a French comedy film (2014):
"Serial bad weddings.
Qu'est-ce qu'on a fait au Bon Dieu?"

What does it mean to you to have your own family?

_ _

Are you happy with your current family circumstances?

_ _

Do you see yourself as a role model to your children?

_ _

Would you like to spend more quality time with your family?

_ _

Would you like to maintain a wonderful relationship with your parents and other family members?

_____

If you have your own family with children, what do you wish for them?

_____

If you are a single mother or father, what is it that you would hope for in any new relationship?

_____

Do you live alone due to separation, divorce, the death of your partner, or because your children have left home? What are you now seeking?

_____

Ask yourself any other question which you consider important, if you have one:

Q: _____

A: _____

My ideal for my family would be:

3) Friendship

Exercise

How important is it to have good friends with which to share your joys and sorrows and to provide each other with mutual support?

_____

_____

What do you seek in a friendship?

_____

Would you definitely choose your current friends again?

_____

Do you consciously make time to spend with your friends?

_____

Do you consider yourself to be a good friend?

_____

What would you like to change with respect to your friendships?

_____

What do you do to make a friendship work?

_____

Ask yourself any other question that you consider important, if you have one:

Q: _

A: _

My ideal friendship would be:

What would be your ideal financial situation?

Exercise

What do you consider you need to be financially secure?

_ _ _ _ _ _ _ _ _ _ _ _ _ _ _ _ _

_ _ _ _ _ _ _ _ _ _ _ _ _ _ _ _ _

_ _ _ _ _ _ _ _ _ _ _ _ _ _ _ _ _

What do you feel when you talk about money?

_ _

Do you feel uncomfortable or do you feel at ease when you speak about money?

_____

What do you actually think about money?

_____

Do you think you deserve financial security?

_____

Do you regularly face financial anxieties?

_____

Do you have a healthy relationship with money?

_____

Do you have a clear financial plan for the next five years?

_____

Do you believe that creating wealth is a good thing?

_____

Why do you want more money?

_____

How would you build up your finances?

_____

Ask yourself any other question that you consider important, if you have one:

Q: _

A: _

My ideal financial situation would be:

What would you wish for concerning your job and or professional career?

Exercise:

What would you consider to be ideal working conditions?

_ _

Is your current career the type of work you enjoy?

_____

Are you happy with what you are currently doing?

_____

Why did you pick the career you are in?

_____

Would you have the courage to change career direction?

_____

If so, what reason would make you take up a new challenge?

_____

What are you really good at?

_____

What would you wish to change about your current career?

_____

What steps would you be prepared to take to make these changes?

_____

Ask yourself any other question that is important to you, if you have one:

Q: _____

A: _____

My ideal job or career would be:

What do you seek with respect to your spiritual life?

Exercise

What does it mean to you to devote yourself to a spiritual practice?

_ _ _ _ _ _ _ _ _ _ _ _ _

_ _ _ _ _ _ _ _ _ _ _ _ _

_ _ _ _ _ _ _ _ _ _ _ _ _

_ _ _ _ _ _ _ _ _ _ _ _ _

_ _ _ _ _ _ _ _ _ _ _ _ _

What is your particular reason for having a spiritual practice?

_ _

Do you seek more emotional stability?

_ _

Do you seek a true purpose in life?

_____

Do you wish to create a different life to the one you live now?

_____

Do you wish to have a deep impact on other people's lives?

_____

Ask yourself any other question which you think important, if you have one:

Q: _____

A: _____

My ideal spiritual life would be:

Chapter 15
Focusing Our Minds in Open Space

Overcoming our monkey mind

Once we have discovered and can envision WHAT we really want, we have taken the first decisive step in making our clear intentions manifest. So, what further steps are required? HOW can we make our wishes come true?

By now it has become clear, that the simple method of chanting Daimoku in fact requires committed and regular practice if we want to attain mastery – just as a commitment to regular training in any art or sport will alone ensure proficiency and success. What is essential is the firm discipline of a steady, regular, and intensive practice with an indomitable spirit to never give up until our goal is accomplished. Even if we have been making efforts in this direction, we may still wonder WHY it sometimes doesn't seem to work out in the way we intend or expect.

In fact, many people quite often ask us the same question. It often sounds like this: "I can't concentrate while chanting and I am always restless because there are so many thoughts and feelings coming and going"; or "I have been chanting in a very intense way and almost make myself hoarse while chanting, but nothing has happened. What am I doing wrong?"

So let's now explore together how we can cope with our monkey mind and improve our ability to focus our attention.

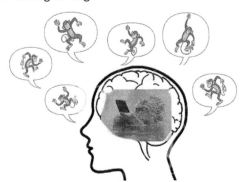

Establishing priorities

We are frequently surrounded by innumerable distractions. There are so many things which demand our attention. If we are constantly adding new things to what we are doing, or if we are constantly thinking about several things at the same time, we begin to feel overwhelmed and our energy is dispersed. In such a state, we send out a weak signal about what we want to the Gohonzon. It is just like a radio signal which jumps between stations, leading to signal interference or distortion.

If we feel overwhelmed by many things which need our attention, we should prioritize according to importance and urgency. For example, we can make a wish list and decide on what to attend to first, as a matter of urgency. Then we should firmly resolve to focus first on the most urgent priority and put the full weight of our commitment behind it.

Exercise: Prioritizing your intentions.

If you don't know which intention or vision is the most important one, you can chant to discover the right answer.

What does your wish list look like?

1. _____

2. _____

3. _____

4. _____

5. _____

Receiving back the energy you emit

Another reason for restlessness while chanting could be because we continue to cling emotionally to things which upset us most of the time. For example, we might be worrying about a certain situation at work, in our relationships, or about our current financial situation, etc. Thus, we might be constantly fluctuating between one thought and another. That´s when we begin to feel overwhelmed and exhausted. For all our negative feelings, such as guilt, hatred, jealousy, fear, our anxieties, regrets, and disappointments, reduce our own energy and disperse it. Thus, it does not make sense to cling to such emotions as they won't provide a solution to the problems we are faced with. Instead of wasting our precious life energy, we need to enhance it and direct our creative power towards a new vision for our future. In order to detach from all current problems and receive back all that energy dispersed among things and people, following exercise might be very helpful.

Exercise

In order to make your intentions manifest while chanting, you need focused attention and enhanced energy. Before you begin to chant for a particular goal, imagine that a magnet behind your eyes is attracting all your energy back to you. Call back all the attention and energy you are giving to the things, people and situations in your external environment.

How do you feel after this exercise? _ _ _ _ _ _ _ _ _ _ _ _ _ _ _ _ _

Focusing our attention by breathing

Harmonious breathing plays an important role both in calming ourselves down and in focusing our mind. To train this capacity try the exercise below before beginning to chant Daimoku:

Exercise

Close your eyes and breath in and out through your nose gently and slowly. Try to breath in deeply down into your abdomen. You can count 1, 2, 3, 4, 5 when breathing in and 1,2,3,4,5 when breathing out. Repeat this cycle of breathing in and out for 5 minutes. Focus your attention only on your

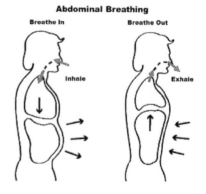

Abdominal Breathing

Breathe In   Breathe Out

Inhale   Exhale

breathing and try to completely detach from any problems which you might be thinking about.

Each time you notice that your attention is going elsewhere and other thoughts are arising, gently bring your focus back to your breathing.

How do you feel after this exercise? _ _ _ _ _ _ _ _ _ _ _ _ _ _ _

As you feel a calming effect on your mind and a stilling of your emotions, you should continue with this exercise for a while.

The necessity of becoming one with the Gohonzon

All the above considerations and exercises are important to help us calm down and free ourselves from an over-active, restless monkey mind. Looked at from a neuroscientific perspective, if we want to enhance the prospect of fulfilling our desires, it is essential for us to calm our mind by changing the electromagnetic pattern of our brain from high-frequency beta brainwave activity to lower-frequency alpha, or even theta or delta, brainwave activity.

Bearing the above in mind, it is very important to once again emphasize how important it is to attain a state of fusion with the Gohonzon, that we earlier described as *"Kyōchimyōgō"*. It is essential to attain such a fusion if we want to fulfil our intentions and actualize our visions as a result of chanting. For *Nam-myō-hō-ren-ge-kyō* is the law of cosmic consciousness which creates all things throughout the universe. Nichiren inscribed his Mandala as a visual representation of its miracle mechanism which we can benefit from. For when we practice the Mystic Law, which means "chanting Daimoku to the Gohonzon," we gain direct access to cosmic consciousness. And it is only at the level of cosmic consciousness, and never at the level of ego- consciousness, that we can activate the miracle mechanism by which we can create the visible from the invisible, or actualize our potential. This is precisely what Deepak Chopra speaks about:

> The only preparation required to unleash the power of intention is a connection to the conscious intelligence field. When a person achieves a certain level of consciousness whatever he or she intends begins to happen. There are people who are so connected to the universal intelligence field that their every intent manifests itself. The whole order of the universe orchestrates around it. The cosmic mind is using their intentions to fulfil its own desires.   - Deepak Chopra

Our intention to fulfill our visions becomes especially strong when unified with the power of cosmic consciousness, represented by the Gohonzon.

When we chant Daimoku, we activate and unfold our true nature and identity. We are transformed in all areas of our life when we chant, as the self which is awakened operates beyond space and time. Imagine this self as the connected self. It is this connection which we have been looking for all our life, seeking to find it through all our relationships, all our activities and in all our possessions. The more we activate and unfold this connected self, the more it becomes manifest in our life and we will discover the place where it is best for us to live, we will find the work that is most meaningful and the relationships which are the most fulfilling. Consequently, we are all challenged to have the courage to connect to our true selves and have confidence in the Mandala Gohonzon, as the means by which we attain to our true nature.

Exercise

Do you trust in the Gohonzon and open up your heart unconditionally? Or do you feel resistant or reluctant to do so?

_ _

Are you willing to become one with the Gohonzon so that you know yourself more deeply thereby becoming more trusting and respectful to yourself?

_ _

How do we keep our attention focused on the Mandala?

Fusion with the Gohonzon is absolutely essential in order to fulfil our visions while chanting. Whenever we merge with the Gohonzon, we merge with cosmic consciousness. All things are created by cosmic consciousness. Nichiren teaches us that Nam-myō-hō-ren-ge-kyō is the law of cosmic consciousness. If we practice this law, then we become active participants in this universal creative process.

Try the following exercise to train your awareness as to how our focused attention functions.

Exercise

Simply try to focus all of your attention on the character of *Myō* or on the *Daimoku* at the center of the Gohonzon, but without chanting while breathing deeply and slowly for 5 minutes!

If you notice your attention going elsewhere and being occupied by other thoughts, gently bring it back to the focus of your attention at the center of the Gohonzon.

- -

How many times has your attention focused on *Myō* been distracted?   - - - -

If you continue with this exercise and write down each day how often your attention has been distracted, you can estimate how much you have been able to develop a more focused attention.

Date	No.	Date	No.	Date	No.	Date	No.
1)		6)		11)		16)	
2)		7)		12)		17)	
3)		8)		13)		18)	
4)		9)		14)		19)	
5)		10)		15)		20)	

How did you feel about the exercise of focusing your attention on the middle of the Gohonzon? Could you bring your attention back to the middle of the Gohonzon? If yes, did you do this in a stressed or in a relaxed manner?

Keeping our attention on the Gohonzon is important. But even more crucial is *how* we intend when we chant to the Gohonzon, i.e. *how* we form and direct our awareness.

The real question is: when chanting, do we adhere ourselves rigidly or flexibly to the Gohonzon?

A narrow attention increases stress

When Nichiren spoke about *"strong faith like a strong bow with a strong bowstring"* (see page 34), he was definitely not talking about a cramped posture. Nor does the term "Ichinen" indicate a fanatical and unyielding "determination", as a strong faith excludes a rigid, stressed or forced manner when focusing our attention.

When chanting, if we focus too narrowly and rigidly in desperation at ever finding a solution to our problems, we will become too hyper-focused and our muscles will be tense. We will remain restless and stressed out, so that we will be incapable of merging with the Gohonzon.

According to Dr. Les Fehmi, a clinical psychologist and researcher in the field of attention and biofeedback training at Princeton University, the way in which we pay attention to a situation or to an object has a measurable effect on our brainwaves. When we narrow our focus, we activate our primordial survival pattern, i.e. our fight or flight response, which causes us to feel intense stress.

The vast majority of us pay attention to our external and internal world in a very restricted, narrow, and tense way, where the focus of our attention is far too cramped. An example of such a narrow attention or focus is when we concentrate on one or more important things in the foreground of our visual field and ignore all the other dimensions of our environment, pushing them into the background of our experience. The narrower our focus is, the more we separate ourselves from our actual environment and the object of our awareness.

Chronic narrowness of attention consumes a great deal of energy and many of us are unaware of the excess stress and tension which a persistent narrow focus will produce. Yet it seems as if we have become used to it. Constantly seeking to maintain such a tense mode of attention, however, necessarily makes us fatigued and ultimately exhausts us. That's when we need a coffee as a stimulant to grab back energy, or a cigarette or a beer to relieve our stress!

If we cannot find relief, stress accumulates and severely compromises our capacities and productivity. Eventually, we are no longer able to concentrate properly, and we begin to feel depressed and anxious unless we can radically shift our mode of attention. Likewise, whenever we are too tense and hyper-focused when chanting, we are chanting with a cramped, narrow focus. That's when our brainwaves remain locked in high-beta and we are stuck in ego-mode. And this stressed out state radically contradicts and undermines the meditative aspect of chanting Daimoku in front of the Gohonzon, which represents the essential unity between each of us and the universe beyond the level of our everyday consciousness. As long as we remain in this high-beta focused state, and we are not able to lower our brainwaves, it is impossible to merge with the Gohonzon. We need to actually lower our brainwaves if we are to become one with the Gohonzon.

A too narrow focus not only distances the observer from the object of awareness but also leads to a stressful high-beta brainwave state. Then we are caught in ego-mode. We need to lower our brainwaves to become one with the Gohonzon.

Exercise

How are you paying attention right now?

☐ I feel restless and uncomfortable.

☐ I place my attention mainly at the center of the Gohonzon and can remain focused.

☐ I place my attention on the whole Gohonzon and can remain focused.

And how do you feel when you place your attention on the Gohonzon in a focused way?

☐ I feel restless and uncomfortable.

☐ I feel emotionally and energetically stressed out, overwhelmed, or bored.

☐ I feel good, vigorous and inspired.

☐ I become fused with the Gohonzon and feel joy and happiness.

☐ etc. _

An open focus dissolves stress

Living constantly in the restrictive, stressful emergency mode of a narrow focus of attention, makes us overreact to almost everything. The habitual attachment to such a narrow mode of awareness separates and isolates us from the world instead of allowing us to merge with it. For example, this can happen if we have an argument with someone. Have you ever noticed that when you are thinking about how someone has hurt you, that's when you only focus on angry feelings and on a sense of being wronged by that other person?

I have often wondered how we might change our mode of attention to over-come the separation be-tween each other and the Gohonzon, so that when we chant we are able to actually merge with it? The answer can be found in cultivating a more open mode of attention with a diffuse focus which gives us a softer, much more inclusive view of the world. It is exactly like focusing the lens of a camera. We can narrow the camera's aperture to get a sharply-focused image of an object or we can widen it to get a panoramic view around an object. So the more we open out our focus, the more we are able to merge with our environment

---

An open focus is an inclusive style of attention that allows both narrow and diffuse forms of attention into our awareness simultaneously.

Being attentive to empty space dissolves stress

Dr. Fehmi discovered that our brain waves will immediately drop into the relaxed state of alpha brainwave, which is the gateway to our subconscious mind, when we widen and diffuse our attention and when we focus also on the space around the object which we are being attentive to. Applying his insight to our Nichiren Buddhist practice, you might try the exercise below, which can help us to sharpen our awareness when chanting Daimoku.

Exercise

Sit upright and relax in front of the Gohonzon. You are now going to take part in the "Ceremony in the Air" as depicted on the Gohonzon. Close your eyes. Imagine you are already in the Air, in the empty space beyond this world.

☐ Can you feel and imagine the space in front of you?

☐ Can you feel and imagine the space behind your body?

☐ Can you feel the space on the right side of your body?

☐ Can you feel the space on the left side of your body?

☐ Can you feel and imagine the space above your body?

☐ Can you feel and imagine the space around your body?

☐ Can you feel and imagine all the boundaries of your body dissolving into the space around your body?

How does it feel to be in and surrounded by empty space?

_____

Do you feel any changes in muscle tension, for example, in your face or in your neck?

_____

A wide-open focus promotes greater brain wave synchronicity which enables us to open ourselves to and to merge with our environment. Research demonstrates that we best attain a more open, diffuse focus if we also place our attention on the space around any object we are focusing on. We can practice this attentive skill in our everyday life and employ it when we place our attention on the Gohonzon while chanting.

Exercise

1. With your eyes open, sit in a gently erect posture while facing the Gohonzon at eye level. Can you *center your attention on "Nam-myō-hō-ren-ge-kyō" in the middle of the Gohonzon* and allow the remaining part of the Gohonzon to become the background to your visual awareness?

---

2. Now try to reverse this process so that you allow the "Nam-myo-ho-ren-ge-kyo" in the middle of the Gohonzon to recede and allow the other inscriptions on the Gohonzon, (*which in exercise 1, you were aware of only in the background*), to move forward in your awareness. What was in the middle is now background. What was background is now at the center of your attention.

---

3. Is it possible for you to give equal attention to the Daimoku in the middle and to the background of the Gohonzon, so that *the whole visual field is viewed equally and simultaneously* with no part of the Gohonzon serving as foreground or background to any other part?

---

4. How does it feel to move out of a narrow-objective focus? Do you feel a relaxation in muscle tension (e.g. especially in your face or neck)?

Chapter 16
Setting the miracle mechanism in motion

Becoming one with everything we do

We need to be in a more relaxed and at the same time focused mode of attention. As a narrow focus puts a distance between us and that which we observe, an open, more diffuse focus allows us to become wholly immersed and to merge and become one with that which is observed. This is precisely the mode of attention that is required if we are to merge with the Gohonzon and to enter into the state of *Kyōchimyōgō,* which we have continuously made reference to above.

This state of mental immersion and concentration resembles that state of a "flow" in which we are completely absorbed in everything that we do. We experience this mode of feeling in any activity which we carry out with intense concentration. Yet in this state, we are no longer simply in in a state of hyper-focus, but we rather enter a trance-like state in which our ego consciousness is absorbed into the vastness of space.

Reminding ourselves again of the example of *"strong faith like a strong bow with a strong bowstring"*, it is well-understood that a Japanese master of archery doesn't deliberately seek to hit a target in the re-mote distance. Ra-ther, he feels him-self to be fused or at one with the tar-get, as if it were immediately and vividly present right before his

eyes so that he can't possibly miss it. This way of practice and performance seems to be uniquely peculiar to the Japanese way of practice in sports such as *Kyūdō* (archery), *Jūdō*, *Aikidō* and even *Sadō* (the tea ceremony) and *Kadō* (Ikebana). In all these sports and arts, practitioners are trained to be at one and in harmonious flow with that which they are doing. And they do cultivate a mental state of hyper-focus, which at the same time is relaxed and in a mode of being free from ego grasping and stress. Such practice techniques ensure that we can enjoy any sporting performance or artistic practice as a kind of meditative practice.

You might have noticed that all the Japanese arts and sports referred to above end with the suffix *"dō"*, signifying the "way" or "path." All Buddhist practice is likewise signified with the same suffix, i.e. by the designation *Butsudō*, which literally means the way of Buddha or to practice in the way of the Buddha. Consequently, we can best characterize our Buddhist practice as below:

Chanting Daimoku represents a meditative exercise characterized by an intense concentration of mind which is at the same time a highly relaxed and joyful mode of being, both in mind and body. We are in a harmoniously flowing relationship with the Mandala Gohonzon upon which we focus while being fully aware of the sacred space which surrounds us.

As many people have recognized the significance of becoming one with the Gohonzon as the primary connection to cosmic consciousness, we are very often asked: "I understand the importance of *Kyōchimyōgō*, but how can I truly enter this state of consciousness? What does it feel like?" The next exercise is designed to improve your ability to enter this state of consciousness and fuse with the Gohonzon.

Exercise

Sit and breath in and out through your nose in a very slowly, gently and deeply. Simply focus all your attention on the character of *Myō* or the *Daimoku* at the center of the Gohonzon. Then begin to chant Daimoku in harmony with the rhythm of your breath! Chant Nam-myō-hō-ren-ge-kyō and imagine yourself merging with the Gohonzon and be aware of the vast, limitless universe contained within your very own body.

Such fusion with the Gohonzon is sometimes accompanied by particular modes of altered consciousness: For example, you might experience 1) a feeling of oneness between your mind and your body, 2) the Daimoku at the center of the Gohonzon may begin to flicker vibrantly, 3) a feeling of joy and immense happiness or limitless gratitude may arise, 4) a feeling of great clarity of mind 5) awareness of a flow of energy ascending from the bottom of your spine up to your upper torso and traversing the front of your body or along the spine itself, or 6) awareness of a flow of energy that descends from your upper body and then flows down through your body.

If you attained to any of the above-mentioned states of feeling or awareness, which should be understood as signs of fusion with the Gohonzon, note how much time you required in order to reach such a state.

How many minutes did it take for you to reach this state? _ _ _ _

At first, you might need more than 30 minutes, but later on it may take you only 5 or even one minute to attain that state beyond your ego mode of consciousness. If you find that this exercise is useful to enable you to focus on the Gohonzon, then you can continue with it for a while.

Exercise

Write down each day how many minutes (x 60 seconds) you required to attain to a feeling of oneness with the Gohonzon. In this way, you can monitor the extent to which you have developed a capacity for focused attention.

Date	*sec.*	Date	*sec.*	Date	*sec.*	Date	*sec.*
1)		6)		11)		16)	
2)		7)		12)		17)	
3)		8)		13)		18)	
4)		9)		14)		19)	
5)		10)		15)		20)	

A profound prayer to activate the miracle mechanism of the universe

In 1273, during his exile on Sado island, Nichiren sent a letter from Ichinosawa, apparently addressed to Shijō Kingo, one of his loyal followers at Kamakura. He ended the letter with the following message.

> No matter how seriously we may face the mess of the world, I turn to the Lotus Sutra and the ten female demons to help all of you. In fact I am praying as earnestly as though seeking to produce fire from damp wood, or to obtain water from parched ground.
> *On Rebuking Slander of the Law and Eradicating Sins*,
> WND I: 444.

During the corona crisis, I have often had the feeling that right now we are actually having "to face the mess of the world". And so did Nichiren in the 13th century. The entire country he lived in was ravaged by natural disasters and civil wars, and his disciples and followers were permanently persecuted and even sometimes killed. Today perhaps our current situation is not as serious and dangerous as it was in Nichiren's time. Yet we have been confronted with the Corona Virus pandemic which has threatened us not only as an infectious pandemic but also in a negative psychological, social and economic way. As most of us have been compelled to remain at home during the time of lockdown, we have sought to provide online Daimoku sessions each evening for several months. In this way, we have been *"facing the mess of the world"* by chanting Daimoku both for ourselves and for all other beings, in order to be free from the negative effects of the virus on our health, emotions, economic situation and general well-being.

During these sessions, we chanted Daimoku with profound sincerity and earnestness, in order *"to produce fire from damp wood, or to obtain water from parched ground."* However, this does not mean that we should "chant with such a determination" as if we have to solve our problems through our own will power and effort alone. For this kind of determined attitude is exactly that type of narrow-focused chanting which ultimately ends only in exhaustion. This way of prayer will almost certainly go unanswered and end in deep frustration.

However, if you read the above quotation carefully, you will become aware of the context Nichiren refers to when speaking of a deep determination to make the impossible possible. He himself turned to the Lotus Sutra and the ten female demons (*Jūrasetsunyo*), the Allies of *Kishimojin*, for help in the fulfilment of his prayers. That is to say, he purposefully activated that cause by which the illuminating power of the Mystic Law, which governs all things throughout the universe, is made manifest, and in so doing, he also ensured the activation of all its supportive functions. Nichiren wants us to understand that by chanting in such a determined and deeply focused way, we can ensure the activation of all those supportive and protective functions and powers throughout the universe which will certainly help and protect us.

Consequently, we do not worship these functions and powers when we chant Daimoku to the Gohonzon. Nor do we ask them for help, either. Rather, we always ensure the *activation* of their protective and supportive function only due to the immense power of the mystic law when we chant Daimoku before the Gohonzon. For the immeasurable power of the mystic law transforms even negative forces and energies into protective and benevolent forces and energies. It can transform darkness into light.

"Praying earnestly as though to produce fire from damp wood"
thus means to chant Daimoku on the firm foundation of
an unshakable trust in the cosmic forces
inscribed on the Mandala Gohonzon.

A meditative exercise to deepen your prayer

This understanding, that you will be supported by the power of Daimoku alone, should help you to free yourself from a narrow and stressful effort to reach your goals. To further assist you with this, we would like to suggest the following exercise in order to improve the way you chant Daimoku in front of the Mandala Gohonzon.

Exercise:

1. Each time when you sit in front of the Gohonzon, close your eyes and repeatedly breath in and out very slowly and deeply for a while, becoming aware of the sacred space which surrounds you. You are about to participate in the Ceremony in the Air.

2. Open your eyes and begin to chant Daimoku, focusing on the Gohonzon. For the first 10 minutes, just keep yourself fused with the Mandala and enjoy the chanting itself in a harmonious, flowing way, full of joy and gratitude.

3. As you are revealing your innermost identity as a Bodhisattva of the Earth, you may become aware of all the cosmic powers surrounding you. At the four corners of your room, the mighty guardians are standing and protecting you from any attacks from outside. Fudo and Aizen are working to enable you to transform your mental and physical sufferings into positive blessings and healing transformations. All other spiritual forces are guiding and supporting you through their great wisdom and profound compassion in order that you may accomplish your visions. You are directly experiencing Nichiren's Mandala world, in that you are connected to all things. You no longer need to worry about anything. You are not alone nor are you missing anything to ensure your happiness and fulfilment.

4. Only after this stage of entry into the Mandala Gohonzon, can you begin to imagine that your visions are already accomplished, as it is at this moment that you enjoy the emotions which you feel as your vision is fulfilled. Express your desires and don't worry about the outcome. But detach from them and remain centered in a state of trustful, open awareness.

At this stage, however, it is quite natural to develop some wholesome plans which would have a positive effect on your ordinary, daily activities.

_ _ _ _ _ _ _ _ _ _ _

_ _ _ _ _ _ _ _ _ _ _

_ _ _ _ _ _ _ _ _ _ _

5. Each time you get a stimulating or insightful idea, it is a challenge to act on it. Never hesitate to continue with this constructive "trial and error" process, as a corrective to your plans.

6. Such a process makes you aware quite naturally of your karmic tendencies, which cause you particular conflict and suffering. Inevitably, you will have to deal with these tendencies as well. You can pray for solutions while trusting in the power of Daimoku. In this way, you will work on the transformation of your karma.

7. At the close of the Daimoku session, you can remain simply enjoying the energy vibrating through your body for a while.

How do you feel now? _

We wish you all success in attaining to the fulfilment of your wishes and visions through the practice of chanting Daimoku to the Mandala Gohonzon!

> Kyō'ō's misfortune should be also transformed into good fortune. Summon a heart of faith and direct your prayer to this Gohonzon with all your energy and focus. Then what is there that cannot be achieved?   *Reply to Kyō'ō*, WND I: 412

References

The following Nichiren-related quotations are based on the *Nichiren Buddhism Library*: http://www.nichirenlibrary.org/en/
LS = The Lotus Sutra
OTT = The Record of Orally Transmitted Teachings
WND = The Writings of Nichiren Daishonin I/II.

Bischof, Marco: *Biophotonen: Das Licht in unseren Zellen*, Zweitausendeins Verlag, Frankfurt am Main, 1995.

Chopra, Deepak, *Das Tor zu vollkommenem Glück – Ihr Zugang zum Energiefeld der unendlichen Möglichkeiten*, München: 2004.

Chopra, Deepak, *Metahuman: Unleashing your Infinite Potential*, New York: Harmony, 2019

Church, Dawson, *Mind to Matter: The Astonishing Science of How Your Brain Creates Material Reality,* New York, Hay House Inc., 2018.

Dispenza, Joe, *Ein neues Ich – Wie Sie Ihre gewohnte Persönlichkeit in vier Wochen wandeln können*, Burgrain, 2012.

Dispenza, Joe, *Becoming Supernatural: How Common People are doing the Uncommon,* Carlsbad, California: Hay-House Inc., 2017

Dürr, Hans-Peter: *Geist, Kosmos und Physik. Gedanken über die Einheit des Lebens,* Amerang, Crotona Verlag, 2013.

Dossey, Larry, *Healing Words: The Power of Prayer and the Practice of Medicine* (New York: HarperCollins, 1993).

Fehmi, Les and Robbins, Jim: *The Open-Focus Brain: Harnessing the Power of Attention to Heal Mind and Body*, Trumpeter Books, Boston, 2007.

Hunt, Valerie: *Bioenergy Demonstration*, https://www.youtube.com/watch?v=_AUqSRVbhC0

Hunt, Valerie: *The Promise of Bioenergy Fields – an End to all Disease*. Interview with Dr. Hunt by Susan Barber: http://www.spiritofmaat.com/archive/nov1/vh.htm

Ikeda, Daisaku: Interview with Mr. Ikeda, "Faith in revolution" by the editors of Magazine TRICYCLE, Winter 2008.
https://tricycle.org/magazine/faith-revolution/

Ikeda, Daisaku: https://www.ikedaquotes.org/human-revolution/
humanrevolution580.html?quotes_start=7

Kabat-Zinn, John: *Gesund durch Meditation*, Frankfurt a.M., 8. Aufl., 2010.

Kattke, Michele: *Intention Power of Consciousness is a Universal Creative Force*: https://www.instagram.com/p/B8cRDhdnPxn/

Kattke, Michele: *Crystallizing consciousness with the universal creative force of intention,* https://www.researchgate.net/ publication/340772456 Crystallizing Consciousness with the Universal Creative Force of Intention

König, Michael, Burnout: *Das quantenmedizinische Heilkonzept*, Scorpio Verlag, München, 2012.

König, Michael: *Der kleine Quantentempel: Selbstheilung mit der modernen Physik,* Scorpio Verlag, München, 2011.

Masaki, Kobayashi and Kikuchi, Daisuke and Okamura, Hitoshi: *Imaging of Ultraweak Spontaneous Photon Emission from your Human Body Displaying Diurnal Rhythm*, PLoS One. Published online 2009 July, 16. Doi: 10.1371/journal. Pone.0006256.

Matthews, Gail: http://www.dominican.edu/academics/ahss/ undergraduate-programs-1/psych/faculty/fulltime/ gailmatthews/researchsummary2.pdf

Lazlo, Ervin: *The whispering pond. A personal guide to the emerging vision of science.* Shaftesbury: Element Books, 1995

Matsudo, Yukio: *Nichiren, der Ausübende des Lotos-Sutra*, Norderstedt 2004 (Taschenbuch 2009). DPI Publishing, 2017.

Matsudo, Yukio: *The Instant Enlightenment of Ordinary People: Nichiren Buddhism 2.0 for the 21st Century.* DPI Publishing, 2017.

Matsudo, Yukio and Matsudo-Kiliani, Susanne: *Transform your Energy – Change your Life: Nichiren Buddhism 3.0.* DPI Publishing, 2016.

Matsudo, Yukio and Matsudo-Kiliani, Susanne: *Change your Brainwaves, Change your Karma: Nichiren Buddhism 3.1.* DPI Publishing, 2017.

McTaggart, Lynne: *Intention. Mit Gedankenkraft die Welt verändern. Globale Experimente mit fokussierter Energie*, VAK Verlags GmbH, Kirchzarten, 2013.

Meijer, Dirk K. F: "*Consciousness in the universe is tuned by a musical master code, Part 1: A Conformal Mental Attribute of Reality*, Quantum Biosystems | 2020 | Vol 11 | Issue 1 | Page 1- 31.

Meijer, Dirk K. F: "*Consciousness in the universe is tuned by a musical master code, Part 2: The hard problem in consciousness revisisted"*, https://www.researchgate.net/publication/338147415

Meijer Dirk K. F.: *Universal Consciousness. Collective Evidence on the Basis of Current Physics and Philosophy of Mind. Part 1.* ResearchGate, 2019.   https://www.academia.edu/37711629/ Universal_Consciousness_Collective_Evidence_on_the_Basis_of_ Current_Physics_and_Philosophy_of_Mind._Part_1

Meijer, Dirk. K. F. and Geesink J.H.: *Is the Fabric of Reality Guided by a Semi-Harmonic, Toroidal Background Field?* International Journal of Structural and Computational Biology, 2018.
https://pdfs.semanticscholar.org/43a5/ dbabe7ce98c06d45451e2329a19327c42dbc.pdf

Meijer, Dirk K.F. and Raggett, Simon: *Quantum Physics in Consciousness Studies:*   file:///C:/Users/SMK/Downloads/ Quantum_Physics_in_Consciousness_Studies.pdf

Mingyur Rinpoche, Yongey: *Buddha und die Wissenschaft vom Glück – Ein tibetischer Meister zeigt, wie Meditation den Körper und das Bewusstsein verändert,* München, 4. Aufl., 2007

Moorjani, Anita: *Heilung im Licht – Wie ich durch eine Nahtoderfahrung den Krebs besiegte und neu geboren wurde*, München, 5. Aufl., 2012.

O'Laoire, Sean: "An Experimental Study of the Effects of Distant, Intercessory Prayer on Self-Esteem, Anxiety, and Depression" in: *Alternative Therapies in Health and Medicine* 3 (1997): 38–53.

Popp, Fritz Albert: *Biophotonen- Neue Horizonte in der Medizin: Von den Grundlagen zur Biophotonik*, Haug Verlag, 2006.

Radin, Dean: *Consciousness and the double-slit interference pattern: Six experiments:*
file:///C:/Users/SMK/Downloads/Radin2012doubleslit.pdf

Schwartz, Gary E.: *The Energy Healing Experiments: Science Reveals our Natural Power to Heal*, New York, Atria Books, 2008.

Schwartz, Gary E.: Integrating Consciousness into Mainstream Science. https://www.researchgate.net/publication/322072255_The_Academy_for_the_Advancement_of_Postmaterialist_Sciences_Integrating_Consciousness_into_Mainstream_Science

Schäfer, Lothar: *Infinite Potential: What Quantum Physics Reveals about How we should Live*, New York, Random House Inc., 2013. https://www.spiegel.de/wissenschaft/mensch/biophotonen-das-raetselhafte-leuchten-allen-lebens-a-370918.html

Tiller, William: *Science and Human Transformation, Subtle Energies, Intentionality and Consciousness*, Pavior Publishing, California, 1997.

Tracy, Brian: https://www.youtube.com/watch?v=M2tgKZLRq3s

Tracy, Brian: *Ziele: Setzen, Verfolgen, Erreichen*. Campus Verlag, Frankfurt, 2018.

Walker, Scott et al.: "Intercessory Prayers in the Treatment of Alcohol Abuse and Dependence: A Pilot Investigation" in: *Alternative Therapies in Health and Medicine* 3 (1997): 79–86.

Winfrey, Oprah: *The Path Made Clear: Discovering your Life's Direction and Purpose*, Melcher Media, New York, 2019.

Worthington, Everett L. Jr.: New Science of Forgiveness (2004). https://greatergood.berkeley.edu/article/item/the_new_science_of_forgiveness

About the authors

Susanne Matsudo-Kiliani, PhD

University degree as translator for English and Spanish, PhD in Translation Studies and Religious Studies specializing in Buddhism, Heidelberg University. Certified trainer for Intercultural Competence in International Business.

Dr. Matsudo-Kiliani has been practicing Nichiren Buddhism since 1998 and has experienced many beneficial transformations in her life, which still continue. As a passionate practitioner she has been engaged in building a bridge between Buddhist practice and modern sciences that are now integrating energy and consciousness.

From 2014-2017 she was a member of the council of the German Buddhist Union (DBU e. V.) and acted as representative for interreligious dialogue at a federal level for a better mutual understanding among different religions.

Yukio Matsudo, PhD

PhD in Philosophy and post-doc qualification for professorship (Habilitation) in the subjects of Japanese Buddhism and Comparative Religions, Heidelberg University.

After receiving his post-doc qualification, he was active as a lecturer at Heidelberg University on the subjects of Japanese Buddhism and Comparative Religions from 2001-2014.

Dr. Matsudo has been practicing Nichiren Buddhism intensively since 1976 and was a top leader of SGI Germany at a federal level until 2001. He has supported hundreds of people in their practice. This way he could also gain many concrete and important experiences.

SGI-President Ikeda asked him personally to found and run as Director of Research *the European Centre of the Institute of Oriental Philosophy* (IOP) in Taplow Court, UK. In this period from 1990-2000, based on the modern, humanistic and open-minded approach of Daisaku Ikeda, he developed an innovative understanding of Nichiren Buddhist teachings and published a number of books and articles in Japanese, German and English.

Today, Dr. Matsudo is engaged in building a bridge between Buddhism, Western philosophy and new scientific disciplines. As an expert in Nichiren Buddhist Studies he is also active in a research group in Japan, in which prominent scholars are represented from all main denominations of Nichiren schools including Soka Gakkai (IOP).

Printed in Great Britain
by Amazon